Testimonials

Inspiring Concepts

"Every now and then we meet someone who is extraordinary. Some of our greatest geniuses have been extraordinary during ordinary times. Andrew Verity is one of these people. His knowledge of the human system goes beyond the usual concepts, his understanding of man's behaviours is inspiring. He is like no other in his field of Neuro-Training. Having lived and worked as an expat in Tokyo, Japan for 18 years I have met many elite people from all over the world in the business sector to artists and Andrew is one of the most inspiring and impressive individuals, and is giving mankind something special to create a better life/future. I have been fortunate to have known Andrew these past few years and received so much knowledge from his teachings and personal training for myself and family that I am ever so grateful for. A huge heartfelt thank you, Andrew. I invite you to be daring and different and challenge yourself to a new adventure."

– Roxy

Physical Integration

"In March 2013, I had a serious accident which left me with a major injury to my right hand, wrist and forearm; including severe nerve damage. After nine months, I had reached a plateau in my recovery. Whilst I had regained most of my sensory range; some numbness remained and I was still physically unable to apply enough pressure to open a door with my hand. I also had restricted mobility of about fifty per cent.

In December 2013, I had the good fortune to meet Andrew Verity in Sydney. After discussing my situation, Andrew very kindly offered to

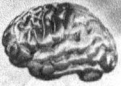

work on my injury. Within fifteen minutes, Andrew had advanced my rehabilitation to the point where I could open a door either way; it was an extraordinary feeling. This feeling, however, was superseded the next morning when I found myself able to take part in a yoga class and do press ups; the sensory ability in my hand fully restored and my mobility elevated to around ninety per cent... In less than one day!!!!

Since Andrew worked his magic on my injury, I now have full use of my previously injured limb. Even the arthritic pain predicted by the surgeon who performed the operation has failed to materialise.

I am eternally grateful to Andrew for applying his knowledge and skills to my predicament. I am particularly thankful for the way in which he approached my situation. Andrew is a patient, positive committed professional who puts his clients first. Without his intervention, I simply wouldn't be where I am today. Andrew's work is a game changer for those in need."

– Emmett McMahon

No more Fear

"I was visiting my mother today and told her about the session you did on me about my fear of tunnels. I told her about the sense of being 'buried alive'. "This has been my deepest fear for the whole of my life". Since your session on me the fear is still gone and I live with your gift every day, thank you so much."

– Torill Osa Michalsen. Norway

For Long Term Issues

"I would highly recommend seeing Andrew Verity he was the one who made the breakthrough for me after 10 years of spending money on chiros, physios (waste of time), and massage, Alexander technique – the list goes on and on. Since 2 years ago I've never had a day off guitar after years of no playing and pain, and it's been beyond life changing! He has also helped me with my back and numerous other things. He will be able to really find out what is going on through muscle testing and his years of experience. Have a few treatments if need be as these problems can be a work in progress. Best of luck!"

– Kieran Larkey

Business Breakthroughs

"I found out Andrew provided consulting services, where I can address all aspects of my life, including and especially work. I was in a situation where I felt I was on a plateau, had peaks and troughs of motivation and had experienced my only loss-making year in 12 years since founding a consulting business. Andrew provided consulting to me for two years. During that time, I significantly lifted my clarity and leadership skills, influence and wellbeing.

Whereas many coaches might use psychological techniques, Andrew works at neurological, physiological and psychological levels – integrating them in a way that allowed me to overcome subconscious blockages. Very powerful stuff, which I translated into action in my businesses to great effect."

– Andrew Hutchinson, Director, Alchemie Consulting

Family Support

"I am a mum of four children, 24, 21, 18 and 10. We have all been having regular balances with Neuro-Training for over a decade. Some of the many benefits have been – the recovery from minor infections is very quick, emotional resilience, reduced allergies and much stronger immune systems. I love the fact that I don't resort to antibiotics – the use of homeopathics has been invaluable. Andrew has guided and taught me so much during the time we've all been seeing him and my children are all now also learning from him and becoming very good at listening to their bodies and the signals it gives them. Our children look forward to each of their appointments and connect with Andrew in a way that helps them navigate their choices and challenges. I have recommended Andrew to many of my friends over the years, who have also had very positive results."

– Fiona Hutchinson

Detox

"Hi Andrew, thanks for your great workshop, I have practiced for 11 days, I now take no more supplements and I feel great. I have a lot more energy. For 5 days I have been doing 'Clean Body' and the red marks in my hands have gone. I lost 2 kg and have much more energy and my whole life is changing. I can now say what I want and what not because I feel much stronger. Thanks for all."

– Silke Digel

Trainer Education

"I get what you are saying. Thanks. In principle, it is simplicity itself, amazing how we complicate things. It certainly has ramifications for how the sessions work and why you have set things up the way that you have. There is a subtlety that I like and find very clever... I will enjoy the new line of thought that has been generated now because of your words. Thanks again, I really do appreciate it.

The nervous system is a powerful and largely untapped resource ready and waiting to help us achieve our dreams. Andrew's passion for research, combined with his ability to design, apply and integrate knowledge into Neuro-Training has seen the development of a modality that speaks the language of the nervous system. Neuro-Training allows us to move beyond, conditioning, limitation and symptoms to live the life we truly desire."

– Jennifer Nelson. Neuron-Training practitioner

The Efficient CEO Brain

GLOBAL
PUBLISHING
GROUP

Global Publishing Group
Australia • New Zealand • Singapore • America • London

The Efficient
CEO Brain

THE ULTIMATE GUIDE TO INSTINCTIVELY
ACHIEVING GREATNESS

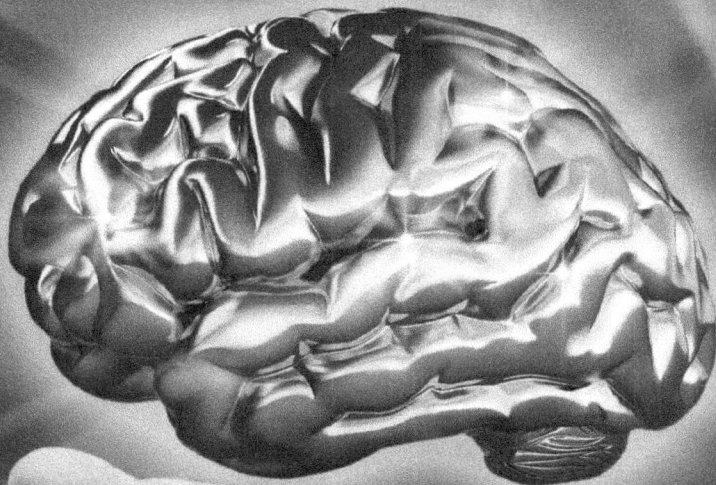

ANDREW D VERITY

DISCLAIMER

All the information, techniques, skills and concepts contained within this publication are of the nature of general comment only and are not in any way recommended as individual advice. The intent is to offer a variety of information to provide a wider range of choices now and in the future, recognising that we all have widely diverse circumstances and viewpoints. Should any reader choose to make use of the information contained herein, this is their decision, and the contributors (and their companies), authors and publishers do not assume any responsibilities whatsoever under any condition or circumstances. It is recommended that the reader obtain their own independent advice.

First Edition 2016

National Library of Australia
Cataloguing-in-Publication entry:

Creator: Verity, Andrew D., author.

The Efficient Ceo Brain : The Ultimate Guide To Instinctively Achieving Greatness / Andrew D. Verity.

1st ed.
ISBN: 9781925288285 (paperback)

Chief executive officers.
Executive ability.
Industrial management.
Leadership.

Dewey Number: 658.42

Published by Global Publishing Group
PO Box 517 Mt Evelyn, Victoria 3796 Australia
Email info@GlobalPublishingGroup.com.au

For further information about orders:
Phone: +61 3 9739 4686 or Fax +61 3 8648 6871

I dedicate this book to the pioneers
and unsung heroes of research for their
contribution to our knowledge of humanity
and its potential. Also to those willing and
brave enough to take that knowledge and
turn into a practical reality. And to those
lucky enough to discover it exists and
experience the massive benefits of being
human to the max!

And to those who learned how to tolerate my
whims, namely my family and friends, who
helped to make Neuro-Training happen.

To the Chief Executive Officers (CEO)
around the world who are constantly and
often without recognition, adding great value
to our lives and to the quality of our planet.

Thank you and keep it up!
Andrew D. Verity

Acknowledgments

I took some time to think about who had been a help or guide or mentor to my pathway to this point in time. The wife of a great internet marketer asked me "who has been the number one helper in your life? Who has given you the greatest consistent support?"

She mentioned we are not islands and even if I think there is no one I would say helped me at that time, we cannot do it alone. It started me thinking about other's contribution to my work. Here, I hope, is an accurate description of those people.

When I think back to when my journey started I would have to say it was my father who initiated my travel in this direction. He has always been an open-minded yet principled reference for me and I thank him for being the one I call my father.

At the time I was playing a massive amount of sport, especially judo, and became friends with a man who had a way of challenging how I thought by being a non-conformist with his own thinking. David Jenkins had qualified as a naturopath and acupuncturist and encouraged me to expand my learning by doing naturopathy, which I did. This opened my eyes to how therapies brought about change in a client's experience through lots of different means. It was here I learned about these principles, so I want to thank those brave, sometimes obsessive compulsive, researchers that discovered them before me.

I started my own clinic, which become the largest of its kind in the southern hemisphere, and where we invited trainers from overseas to come and expand our knowledge. One such teacher was Gordon Stokes, from Three In One Concepts. Even though I didn't know it at the time,

he became my greatest mentor and influence in forming a mindset about what I did in helping others. He was a very understated but insightful human being to whom I owe the greatest debt of gratitude. I still miss him to this day.

I want acknowledge one person who shares still my ideas and aspirations, Jennifer Beasley, who has been with me in many types of relationship, and we care for the work that has proven itself over the decades, against many odds.

In the development of Neuro-Training we had a number of students who were dedicated (still are) to 'getting it out there' and who formed themselves together to create an executive board. My first sponsor – Geraldine Gallagher – and Valery Walters, Philip Man, Penny Carrier, Coleen McClymans, and Dana Hookins. As it continued to develop, with the help of the executive, the College of Neuro-Training was formed. Especially helpful were Valery Walters and her daughter Caroline – thank you.

Now the college is represented in many countries in Europe and Africa and to those brave pioneers who took on the job of establishing the college, my sincere thanks for your integrity and perseverance. Kari Weium, Torill Osa Michalsen, Fabrizio Leo, Silke Digel and other sponsors over the years, too many to name. To the many hundreds of students and thousands of clients over the years, thank you for being my research material and willing to listen to me rant and rave, I really appreciate you!

Special thanks to Estefania Rieder Batista, who shook my tree and watered it at the same time. Who supported and challenged me for the last 12 years to be a better man.

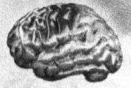

And I know it sounds lame, but I want to thank my kids who had to take second place to workshops and travel and who still loved me just the same. You mean the world to me and I love you very much, thanks for being you.

FREE BONUS GIFTS
Valued at $2146 - But Yours <u>FREE</u>!

Claim your FREE bonus gifts by going to:

www.TheEfficientCEOBrain.com

The Business of Business is to stay in Business but the Business of Greatness is to create Greatness for you and others. Here are the tools you will need to start the process and build that greatness instinctively.

To get you moving I want to give you these bonuses especially suited to your ongoing influence over yourself and the world. Mastery is one thing, but taking that to the world in the right way is greatness.

They will be downloaded to your computer within seconds of registering your copy of this book.

You will receive:

- *Short and precise videos for each of the techniques listed in this book.* **Valued at: $459**

- *A PDF guide of the processes so you can keep your eye on the ball, with its own scheduling format to keep you accountable.* **Valued at: $157**

- *Yours only, Greatness Acceleration Call with me, so we can establish a compatible program for your business or project. Remember this is not a business consulting call. It's a 'you becoming great' call. Up to one hour.* **Valued at: $479**

- *Free access to the Adaptive Neurology Webinar, explaining how to apply your new knowledge of how you really operate. Learn how to create what you want in life the easy way.* **Valued at: $397**

- *Applied Personology Training Live or DVDs. An added training on understanding what your face traits tell the world about you and how you can understand a person better than they can themselves.* **Valued at: $427**

- *And I want you to have no Fear in any of these processes so I'll give you a DVD training video on how to destroy fear and keep the energy. 'Being Better Than Fear' DVD for free!* **Valued at: $227**

Total Value: $2146

Claim your FREE GIFTS TODAY and start the building of the world you always imagined possible by visiting

www.TheEfficientCEOBrain.com

Contents

Preface

For over 40 years I have been involved in the alternative health industry and I still marvel at how the human body can adapt to the degree it does. Even where the treatments given range from completely irrelevant and mediocre to downright dangerous, it still survives the best way it knows how.

The greatest I found, was to be able to find the best treatment for a person, not just a better one.

To this end I have put together a modality which is based on proven principles from the human sciences, health, personal development, physics and neuroscience. These principles have been a guiding force for me and have allowed me to create a set of working models that can address the means for anyone's recovery from the challenges they have.

The learning I have obtained in this process has been remarkable in a number of ways. Humans are indeed remarkable adaptive machines that can take advantage of just about any resource we throw at them. They do so much better when the resources are also based on universal principles and can create new options through natural procedures. Even though the procedures may be predictable, the end results are different for each person.

Understanding these principles and procedures has become my life task and I enjoy completely this journey of discovery.

This is the first book of many, I am sure, which will present the learning I have obtained by observing, challenging and experimenting with people for over four decades. It's a pleasure for me to be able to share this information, because it is so fascinating to discover the understanding of how we really operate and learn how to put that into practice.

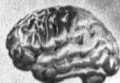

Hopefully it doesn't take you 45 years to get it right, and with me blazing the trail so to speak, you can have the advantage of use of resultant Adaptive Neurology.

- I want you to find an understanding of how you operate at a very intrinsic level, and how to influence that operation with whatever it takes to get it right.

- To learn that getting it right doesn't have to take years but can be brought into play extremely quickly. As quickly as you let it.

- And a proper context is more important to your nervous system than the elimination of symptoms for comfort sake.

> **"If you want something you've never had, you need to do something you've never done."**

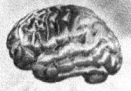

Introduction

Welcome to this book which has been carefully designed to help CEOs and senior managers on getting the most out of their brain, and most importantly of all, to understand how to unlock a natural power and harness methods of tuning your thinking to help you achieve greatness.

Sounds a bit far-fetched and dramatic? It really isn't, and although the brain is by no means a simple subject, there are some fairly simple techniques which will help you focus your mind and unlock its immense power to your advantage.

Now, you are probably not looking to become a brain surgeon or neurologist by reading this book, but the whole concept becomes much easier to understand and use if you have a basic comprehension of how the brain works and what I mean by Neuro-Training, an area I have been developing for many years. This is explained as simply as possible in Chapter 1.

In Chapter 2 we look at what I call the Model of Universal Principles (MUP), which is a model I have developed to help us understand our subconscious, at least in a very small way. As you will learn, our subconscious really can be 'a mind of its own' if left to its own devices. We also take a look at your 'Survival Code' and how important our nervous systems are in learning to control our subconscious.

Chapter 3 continues the theme with a more in-depth look at the MUP model, a little more about the basics of Neuro-Training and also a look at some of the potential pitfalls for a CEO such as depression and stress, including the aptly named CEO Depression Syndrome or CDS.

In Chapter 4 I take the opportunity to draw on my emotions and experience that I have gained through my professional life, as a way of explaining why I am so excited and dedicated to the MUP model and Neuro-Training, amongst other neurological theory, as a way of training our minds and really achieving the best we can achieve in our careers when so many people depend on us.

Chapter 5 looks deeper at our attention spans, our subconscious, brain integration and even what makes certain CEOs excel in their careers. We also look at uncertainty and decision-making and demonstrate why it is possible for us to train our brains to work with us, i.e. Neuro-Training.

Chapters 6 and 7 provide you with the exercises and training methods which really do help you train your brain and nervous system! This is the Neuro-Training gym complete with personal trainer and will help you train your brain, nervous system and genetic system to achieve greatness.

Dealing with stress is of mandatory importance for being a great CEO and also an area where Neuro-Training principles can help. Although our aim here is really to use Neuro-Training and the philosophies outlined in this book to adapt and avoid creating stress in the first place, rather than using this information as a cure from an already stressful situation.

> **"The journey of a thousand miles begins with one step."**
>
> Lao Tzu: 604 BC -531 BC, Henan, China.
> The Book Of Tao Te Ching.

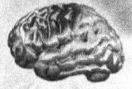

No doubt you have seen this quote before from Lao Tzu, but have you ever wondered why it takes a thousand miles? I guess the message is trying to point out that to achieve great results you have to take that first step, right? The assumption is that the journey will be a thousand miles long! But the blinding flash of the obvious is the first step was taken in **the wrong direction! Heading in the right direction is everything. So this proverb has a secondary assumption we always overlook!**

As a CEO you are told the most powerful resource you have is your Mind. But then the techniques you are given send you off in the wrong direction. No wonder it takes so long to achieve what really could have been just around the corner. The Ideas, Concepts, Perception and Strategies may sound good for the sake of the journey but in terms of speed of result, probably a little off!

You are told to take Action before anything can be achieved. You will find out but the hard way whether an action is good or bad by the results you get (ROI). You learn about the consequences of the change by feedback from the outside world. The amount of good change is proportional to the quality of the feedback. And yet you have never been trained to take the right action beforehand so it's always an 'after the event' scenario. That takes a long time out of an already short enough journey – life.

What we are told by Personal Development and Business Training	The resultant experience from Neuro-Training
MIND	**SUBCONSCIOUS**
Tells	Forms
⬆⬇	⬆⬇
BRAIN	**NERVOUS SYSTEM**
Habitual Survival	Competent Choice
⬆⬇	⬆⬇
ACTION	**MUSCLE MOVEMENT**

I want to introduce you to Neuro-Training. To become familiar with what it can do for you, let's have a look at this overview of how the 'internal pathways' of our mind works; See above. We have two parallel pathways in our psyche that we need to know about and we also need to understand how to make them work together seamlessly. The consequence of proper intervention in the brain forms these pathways into a set of neurological connections which become the code for success. Success then is a consequence of brain and nervous system activity which creates the right connections for the desired outcomes, not just 'any' connections.

If we leave it up to 'good luck', these two pathways inevitably become more and more incoherent and create more conflict rather than

successfully achieving our goals. Many factors need to be considered to make the integration a useful tool for directing our lives and companies.

The Mind's Internal Pathways

The main difference between these two pathways is what we consciously take in (on the left side of the chart), Mind to Brain into Action – how we develop a conscious awareness of life and ourselves in it. The effect of this pathway is to create for us a sense of our reality or an interpretation of the events in life as they create the external reality. It's here we think we live and it's here we create our personality and sense of what works and what doesn't work in life.

The Subconscious, Nervous System and Muscle Movement pathway is the HOW we carry out the other pathway, but also how we do our internal processing. The Mind tells the Brain and the Brain constructs our actions by influencing the muscle responses to support the needed action.

Actually both pathways meet at the muscle activity level and it's here we get access to both pathways if we know how to do it. (Which we do, by the way!) Neuro-Training accesses the activity of both pathways through monitoring the changes of response in the muscle system as a feedback to conflict between the two pathways.

How this relates to your business is quite remarkable. You are the driving force in your business and it needs your energy and engagement to make it follow the desired direction for success. If your pathways are in conflict, then the results in your business will reflect that same condition. Remember both pathways are bi-directional and influence the complete pathway not just one section of it.

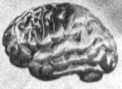

That means if you are not clear at any one level, it still affects the rest of the pathway. It is extremely important that for you to be the success you know you can be that these pathways are monitored for any internal unresolved conflict.

A resolved conflict goes into the memory banks and is used as a resource, but unresolved issues, no matter how long ago or deeply buried and kept away from our conscious awareness they may be, still influence these pathways and create a kind of background noise. This noise will build over time and create what we commonly call sabotage and failure.

Resolution creates competence instead of having to battle through habits outside of our conscious awareness. We need then to check that our conscious direction is in line with the subconscious response to that direction. There are times when our goals are just not the right ones, no matter how plausible they sound. The question is how would we know this situation exists? Via checking the pathways for conflict relating to that goal. Your subconscious responses will show where a goal is just plain wrong. And it will show where your goals are worth pursuing.

Emotions are the motivation and energy required to run this whole system. A Great CEO has an emotional association to each of these three levels of function. The Master CEO has the RIGHT emotions associated to these three levels of functioning.

Neuro-Training Creates Master CEOs.

Waiting for change to happen from ineffective and sometimes wrong feedback wastes too much time and resources. Neuro-Training identifies the right feedback and implements it straight away, by associating it to the nervous system's current desired outcome. The result has proven to be so much faster and so much more efficient.

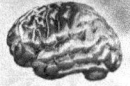

Are you the CEO? This book will provide you with the knowledge and the control over your body and mind which will result in you becoming instinctively successful and respected as a leader.

Andrew Verity

Neuro-Training uses the muscles and nervous system as the feedback device to give instant internal monitoring to know what the right action is, and then to take that action as if it were already a natural function. This can be done easily without having to force anything into submission.

Developing power not force.

One of the keys to success is using the nervous system to tell us when we go into survival mode rather than creating Competence, the most highly-paid human characteristic on the planet. Once we have found how to be competent we then just need the energy to drive it.

Associating new options with the nervous system becomes a new habit and develops your own efficient CEO Brain.

Aimed directly at the CEO or the responsible decision-maker in any business or organisation, this book will provide you with the knowledge and the control over your body, brain and mind connections which will result in you becoming instinctively successful and a respected business leader.

Have you ever put on an old jacket and found hundreds of dollars inside the pocket, or picked up a book and opened it to find that winning lottery ticket that you thought you had lost?

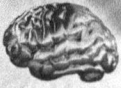

Do you remember that feeling? How about the time your best friend showed up at your door just when you were wondering what you would do that day? These good feelings somehow had their seed in good luck right?

Well, that's exactly how I felt, and still feel today, about finding my way into Neuro-Training. Through it I discovered Adaptive Neurology as a way of discovering I had more control over my mind and body than I could ever have imagined, and I am grateful for the 40+ years it took me to get here and that the journey is nowhere near finished.

The 'future shock' in realising its potential and how it could benefit everybody on the planet was a true revelation to me, and now it's time that this information becomes available to everybody, so you can discover the positive effect it can have on your life. I am privileged to be instrumental in your journey to discovering this amazing personal resource – **Adaptive Neurology**.

Many people have asked me why I started this journey into the realms of the mind and nervous system. I think the real answer is that I saw within its depths a great simplicity and what I learned in NLP as a "Blinding flash of the obvious!" It just made so much sense to me that this was an amazing but normal phenomena that had the potential to help everyone, and had somehow been completely overlooked. The moment I saw it work, I felt a jolt in my brain that said this is it! This is what I must know and, as a consequence, I have been studying and researching it ever since.

It would be many years and thousands of clients later that I really discovered the importance of Adaptive Neurology, and this awareness has become greater the more I learned about it. It has taught me how people operate on a daily basis and how positive long-term change is a myth while we habitualise all the wrong stuff! Understanding what

forms the mind's perception of the world – rather, your world – is a key to being free from the struggle we create between what we want and what we have made already.

The 'why' became much deeper and revealed itself as a way of giving back independence and freedom to the individual in a climate where we are lead to believe lies about ourselves and encouraged to stay within the system for our own good. Understanding how we process life internally has become the basis of most personal development tools today.

I do believe Adaptive Neurology is a better option, and even though you may have not experienced it for yourself yet, I hope I can explain it for you so you end up at the same conclusion.

The real 'why' of this is to train the nervous system to become a design tool, a recuperative mechanism and a resource far beyond what we would normally be led to believe is possible.

I wondered what circumstances must be in place that would demand such a potent tool to become available on the planet? The answer is a little abstract for some and downright ridiculous for others, but in fact it's actually affecting all of us in different ways.

The answer is Suppression

Humans are very expressive animals and we have to express ourselves in many different ways in experiencing the scope of what life has to offer. Do we actually get to have that experience, or are we seconded into living a lifestyle which substitutes what we really want with a 'good enough'? Society is formed around certain principles, some of which are in line with our needs and others to create needs for us. Either way, we end up compromising rather than designing our lives.

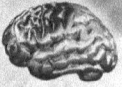

This inability to create a life by design is a form of suppression. We will probably suppress ourselves, along with a hand from others as well. Government seems to have the exclusive rights to create more and more rules that supress the freedom of the individual each minute.

I had a terrible thought some time back while I was sitting enjoying nature. As I pondered how nature has a natural plan for everything it does, I wondered what would happen to me if I was to be hit by a car and knocked unconscious. What would happen? I would have no control over the events that followed and my life would be in the hands of people I wouldn't even know. They could do what they liked to me and I would have no say in the direction of events that followed.

I know it sounds a bit paranoid but in reality this is exactly what happens. It's a little naive to believe that everyone is here to help us for the sake of helping, or to believe that society is constructed as an aid to an individual's needs. And it's even more scary to realise that we live in a world that has made more progress in the sciences than at any other time in history, yet we still allow others to kill each other, allow children to die for lack of food, allow insanity to rule through our governments while we have more than enough resources to make the required changes to make it right!

So is science really our friend or a tool used by society to justify its own needs? When I look at the clients I have had over the last 30 years it occurs to me that the greatest obstacle to health these days are the treatments handed out at great expense that are either ineffectual and or more lethal than the maladies they claim to cure. This kind of activity is another form of suppression and one that has dominated our understanding of health for too many decades.

Any activity, no matter where it comes from, that takes away a person's ability to express their needs sincerely is a form of suppression. When

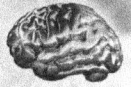

circumstances determine that you are to be 'processed' in a certain way outside of your consent (it is assumed you give consent if you are unconscious), this must be a form of suppression.

What this means to us is that we have to learn how to adapt in the best way possible to survive the threats, and the possibility of loss of our freedom. Unfortunately, as long as we live in a society that has its basis in money we will forever be compromising our lifestyle for survival.

To reveal this information, I had to make a decision, either to be straightforward and offend some people, or become a politician and deliver the ideas in such a way that you would have to work out the truth for yourselves. I chose the direct approach as it seemed to me there are already too many politicians in our lives. Besides, the truth will hurt those who are lying to themselves so I hope this serves as a wakeup call for a few people (well, many people really).

A lot of independent people have learned to play this game of survival very well and they set the pace for us by how well they succeed or fail. These are the entrepreneurs, thought-provokers and leaders, without whom we wouldn't know how to better our own life experiences. We owe a debt of gratitude to these people who learn to go outside of the conformities and challenge themselves to make a better way possible.

It's for these people I write this book as a contribution to their cause in a way that I know will bring about a new way of viewing, thinking and understanding of how humans live.

Context and the survival of the species!

We play a role in carrying out what the brain wants to achieve. It's true, even though we think we are in charge of what we want, the brain and subconscious have their own agenda.

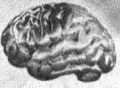

Take the speed of speech as an example. Research has shown that words are formed in our brains seconds before we become aware of those words. It makes me wonder who is running the show really. Where do the thoughts live that create the wording before we come to know what is being created in our minds and ultimately communicated?

It's just another fact demonstrating how the brain works versus what we think we know about ourselves. Maybe we will never truly know all there is to know about how the brain works but we can certainly test its abilities and train it to become more efficient at doing what we want it to do.

Firstly, let's have a quick view of a trend we need to understand better; brain science is persistently championed as an answer to life's deepest problems. It reveals "the deepest mysteries of what makes us who we are", claims Elaine Fox in the introduction to her book *Rainy Brain, Sunny Brain*, which could be the introduction to any number of pop neuroscience books that now fill our shelves. *Super Brain, Buddha's Brain, The Tell-Tale Brain, The Brain that Changes Itself* – you could stock a library with the new generation of books which encourage us to view life through a neurological lens.

I'm certainly not suggesting that this book will solve your life's deepest problems, but I am suggesting that by taking control of your own neurological system you can train your brain to adapt, to think differently and to design your life and the way you want to operate.

During your journey with me you will discover:

- How to double the energy you devote to running the show when you need it. Have energy on tap.

- How to create certainty of mind in all your business decisions.

- Your personal psychology of doing what's right.

- How to create breakthrough systems and structures 'out of the blue'.

- How to break through company politics with relevant and unique communication.

- Five key health practices mean you will never worry about your health again.

- How to smash through the, "Nobody can do it better than me", syndrome.

- How to tap into learning and processes of change for success.

- Your essential position with money to attract investors and clients to accelerate your growth.

- Insider secrets to keeping your brain working at 100% to produce clear, sharp, clever decisions.

- Shortcuts to being great even though you do it easier than anyone else.

- How your focus can make it easier to make more than staying at the level you are now.

- How to empower your future by applying Adaptive Neurology.

- How to guide others to a better future with your influence.

Chapter 1

WHAT IF YOUR MIND DOESN'T MIND?

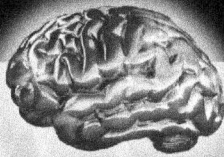

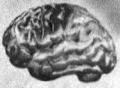

Chapter 1

WHAT IF YOUR MIND DOESN'T MIND?

> "Knowing others is intelligence;
> knowing yourself is true wisdom.
> Mastering others is strength;
> mastering yourself is true power.
> If you realize that you have enough,
> you are truly rich."
>
> Lao Tzu, *Tao Te Ching*

What will you achieve from reading this book? Firstly, this book is not about intelligence, Business Strategies or Techniques, a new social religion or a new 'brain' science.

Finding true power within yourself by understanding mastery is what I want for you and this book holds the keys to doing that.

> "When I let go of what I am, I become what I might be."
>
> Lao Tzu.

Let's see how!

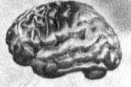

Train Your Brain in a Way It Understands

This book is '*simply*' about the relationship between the brain and the body. I use the term 'simply' loosely as it's not a simple subject, which is why I have spent many years working on and developing the most effective way of simplifying and passing on this critical information so that you can benefit and apply it in your position as CEO in your organisation.

I have specialised in natural medicine of various types for over 40 years and have built a reputation as an innovator in the area. I also direct a Government recognised College of Neuro-Training which now has campuses in Australia, Norway, Italy, Germany and South Africa and is practiced in many more countries.

I have been instrumental in establishing associations and regulatory bodies in the industry, as the president of various associations including the International Association of Specialized Kinesiologists (IASK) as well as developing the Diploma of Solution Oriented Neuro-Training and I will continue to develop Neuro-Training as an enhancement tool in the area of Research and Integral Recuperation.

So, let's start by explaining what Neuro-Training is, and how it relates to you as a CEO or senior director in a business.

Understanding Neuro-Training

All your life you have been conditioned to respond in certain ways. These responses have accumulated over the years to the point where you are now the person you are because of your conditioning. This conditioning comes in two main forms, the first is your genetic material with all of its quirks and fancies, and the second is your learned reactions to life's challenges. In all of your experiences it has been your nervous system

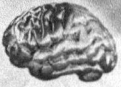

that learned how to carry out those responses and reinforce them as habitual behaviours.

A primary focus of Neuro-Training is to be able to help you change existing conditioning that is limiting the potential for you to create the business you want, and to express who you truly are. Such conditioning initiates habitual responses and therefore activates subconscious references for how we 'do' life. Changing habitual responses changes the conditioning and retrains the nervous system to create better options. New options free more energy and create different response patterns to challenges, freeing you to change response/conditioning creating the ability to 'live' the life you choose rather than merely 'survive'.

Neuro-Training is a 'hands-on' modality which utilises the principles of other proven health, personal development and human sciences to train the nervous system through the process of Adaptive Neurology. This is achieved through activating the innate systems within you to function better, by training the nervous system to become more competent and create the best neurological connections.

Adaptive Neurology is where you use a number of references that direct your nervous system in any new adaption. If the relationship between the nervous system and these references is compromised the result will be compensation and incompetent function. Neuro-Training identifies when your Adaptive Neurology is unable to access or use the appropriate references, and then reassociates the neurology to the most appropriate reference. This phenomenon of neurological association allows Neuro-Training to add better options to the nervous system and how it operates naturally.

Neuro-Training finds any adaption that is not the best for you at any time or in any circumstance and can find the best way for you to change the old adaption into the best adaption. When you 'adapt' badly the

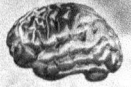

result is better described as 'compensation'. All compensations require energy to maintain them, while an adaption creates more energy either by releasing existing compensations (freeing energy) or establishing processes that create more energy. This is a bridge building operation and the neurology is working more efficiently when bridges are being made.

> **"Neuro-Training gives you the ability to achieve any level of development you wish."**
>
> Andrew Verity

Neuro-Training is also used to find the best types of challenge for the client and then train their nervous system to overcome those challenges in the most competent way. The Adaptive Neurology then becomes stronger and becomes an ongoing developmental process within the nervous system and brain. The result is the client starts to look for bigger and better challenges.

As Sir Richard Branson said to a colleague of mine, "If you want to overcome a problem, make a bigger problem and solve that!"

Neuro-Training helps those clients who are constantly compensating (session clients) while trying to become more competent at resolving their immediate issues, as well as those people already adapting better than average (consultant clients) who want to become more competent by overcoming bigger challenges. The progression from a session client to that of consultant client should be a natural transition and growth process.

Neuro-Training gives you the ability to achieve any level of development you wish.

You may not be so interested in the workings of the brain, but I strongly suggest you engage in this section because it highlights behaviours you may want to catch yourself doing and change them.

Our brain – in a nutshell

The two hemispheres make up the neocortex mentioned above. Basically, you have two brains that come from your genetic blueprint, the left brain you could describe as the logical brain and the right brain which is more the overseeing, imaginative brain.

As two separate entities they are in constant conflict and competition with each other for a number of different reasons.

For a start, the left brain is where you develop your sense of personality. It's where you understand who you are, if you like, the place where you keep your 'self-image', especially in a language form.

It struggles every day to protect that 'self' at all costs. That means it will divert energy, attention and ability towards protecting you when it thinks you are under any threat that would alter that image.

Remember, it is also here on the left side that your major language processing is initiated.

The other 'half' of the brain I find to be a bit more interesting as it has some very different qualities to it. This side looks at the bigger picture of where everything fits together, regardless of your 'self-image'. It's from here you can even change your 'self-image', if the two sides of the brain would work together.

It also exercises its ability to challenge what you think about yourself and life. It is the part of your brain that will create the life traumas and

reality attacks that ultimately have the greatest learning and change attached to them.

Why would the sides of our brains not want to work together?

The 'reptilian brain' is the primitive part of the brain and is the major 'survival expert' of the nervous system. It is reflexive and has great influence over the mechanisms that relate to the survival response.

When the reptilian brain is in survival mode, it turns on mechanisms that change how you operate internally. It stimulates the release of hormones and chemicals that changes blood distribution, blood pressure, digestion processes, muscular activity and a host of other systemic responses.

It has links to 'higher' parts of the brain to carry out these changes, but these changes will not be done if the reptilian brain says, "you are in a threatening situation here".

The more times the reptilian brain 'kicks in' and influences the other mechanisms in the brain, the more habitual responses we develop. The stronger these habits become, the more the two sides of the brain are polarised and become independent of each other.

The scientific community is doing a lot of great research into how the brain works. We are privileged to be in a place in history where this research is developing at the fastest rate ever experienced. Part of that development comes from the study into consciousness and the Neuro-Sciences that have developed as a consequence of achieving this goal.

Survival Brain, or else!

The survival response has become extremely sophisticated over the history of human development, while maybe some other abilities have been regarded as a consequence of this survival habit.

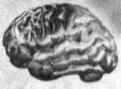

The left brain is already designed to act in your best interest against threats of various types. When you perceive you are under attack, the brain works to reorganise your energy to move into the body to support its need to fight or run from the threat.

If the right brain is trying to do something else at the time, it is simply disconnected, via a structure called the corpus callosum. This is the main connection hub between the two sides. The left brain can and often does restrict the communication from the right side because the left is too busy 'surviving' to pay attention the what the right is saying.

This is good if you need to fight off an enemy or run from a dinosaur, but not good when the dinosaur is a tax notice or a letter from the divorce solicitor.

When your response is disproportionate to the need, the response becomes a handicap to you. It then becomes habitual over time and an unchallenged part of your behaviour.

You then spend most of your time in a defence state, having to 'survive' most things.

Stress is a brain splitting process.

I just mentioned the left and right brains as separate entities. But the sides of the brain by themselves do not determine what type of stress you will experience.

There are two critical factors in how you produce stress.

One: Which Side. The 'Dominance' of the brain hemispheres has a great influence on what type of stress will be acted out by your subconscious.

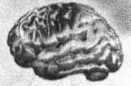

The 'Dominance' is the side of the brain you tend to use as the 'Initiator' of any action or function. This means the dominant hemisphere acts as a contextual director of the activities you engage in, even if you don't know that consciously.

If the right brain is dominant when you go into a stress reaction, it exercises the characteristic of 'Challenging' what is happening. Or, it might use 'Escapism' (flight) as its preferred defence because these are right brain characteristics.

If the left brain is initiating the defence, the person tries to 'Attack' (fight) verbally or physically or uses 'Logic' as its preferred weapon.

Two: What that side does. The second critical factor is the initiation of the response from the dominant brain hemisphere. You see, the reptilian brain is what activates the stress reaction, but the dominant brain determines what type of stress reaction will be acted out.

Humans inherit the processes of defence which appear in the left hemisphere. This means most people (over 80%) are automatically 'programmed' to react from their left brain, therefore from the 'attacking' position. Even if you were doing a right hemisphere activity when you 'were threatened', most of us would naturally initiate how we acted out a stress response from our left hemisphere.

This attacking response is totally socially unacceptable, so what do you do with this stress reaction?

You internalise it, most of the time, until you can't hold it in anymore and your behaviours reflect your stressed state.

In summary; the left brain stressed people will try to 'fight back' first as a defence.

A typical statement they would typically use is, "Oh well, I will just have to work/fight harder!"

The right brain stress people will try to escape or pretend there is no problem at all (Denial or Amnesia). Their typical statement would be, "Time heals all wounds". While they simply pretend there is no stress, until the physiological impact starts to change their internal functions and symptoms start.

It doesn't really matter what the 'pattern' of your stress is, but the habituating of it does matter.

The reptilian brain tells the rest of the brain it is under threat, the dominant hemisphere takes over to produce the reaction and every time you do that you make the stress reaction stronger and habitual.

The Reticular Activating System (RAS)

We have looked at some of the mechanisms within the brain that maintain your ability to make the reaction. We have noticed that this reaction can become a habituated activity to the point where the person does the stress reaction in preference to any other response.

Now, let's have a look at something called the Reticular Activating System, (RAS which is much easier to remember).

Do great leaders possess higher thinking skills? Probably not, but if you want to be a leader — the sort of manager that people admire — you need to use your entire brain! This applies to the stress aspects too, and believe it or not, even the reptilian, survival-oriented section of your brain can make you into a better CEO, leader or manager.

The RAS is the portal through which nearly all information flows into the brain, with the exception of smells which go directly into your brain's

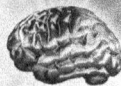

emotional area. Your RAS filters incoming information and basically decides what you pay attention to, how aroused you are, and what is not going to get access to your brain. Sort of a Personal Assistant-gatekeeper.

For survival's sake, your RAS responds to your name or personal information or anything that might threaten your survival. It also picks up on information that you need immediately or are looking for. For instance, if you're scanning through hundreds of filenames in a list, your RAS alerts your brain to search and recognise the name of the file or focus on one word in the filename which will 'jump out' at you once you see it.

Your RAS also responds to anything new and different. In terms of leadership, this means noticing anything unusual or unexpected during the day-to-day running of a business or operation, attending to changes in production, employee moods, and interactions with others.

Your RAS is a great leadership tool, your radar detector and early warning system, as well as your brain's PA. We will come back to this later on as part of our Neuro-Training exercises.

Focused Leadership – how your frontal lobes play a role

Ask most leaders, and you'll probably get the same answer; that the main leadership function is to direct attention (in you and in others), and to do so leaders must learn to focus their own attention. When we use the term 'focused', we normally refer to concentrating on one thing while filtering out others. However, there is a huge amount of recent research in neuroscience which shows that we, as humans, can focus in many ways, for many different purposes whilst drawing on many neural pathways—some of which work together, while others tend to stand in opposition.

We can group these modes of attention into three distinct areas; focusing on yourself, focusing on others, and focusing on the wider world. This research has actually shed new light on the practice of many essential leadership skills. For example; focusing inwardly and focusing constructively on others, helps leaders cultivate the primary elements of emotional intelligence. A broader understanding of how to focus on the wider world can improve the ability to develop strategy, be innovative, and manage people and organisations.

Every leader needs to develop these three areas of awareness in large amounts, but in a balanced way. Failure to focus inward leaves you without direction, a failure to focus on others renders you ignorant, and a failure to focus outward is likely to leave you exposed.

Self-Awareness

Emotional intelligence begins with self-awareness or 'getting in touch with your inner voice', to coin a well-used term. It's generally acknowledged that leaders who listen to their inner voices can draw on more resources, make better decisions and connect with their real selves. This is all very well but how do you do this? Let's take a look in a bit more detail and then we will come back to this later as part of our Neuro-Training.

By paying close attention to internal physiological signals, we are able to hear our 'inner voice'. The insula, which is tucked behind the frontal lobes of the brain, is where these subtle signals are processed. When we pay particular attention to any part of our body, our insula's sensitivity is drawn to that part. If you tune in to your heartbeat, the insula will normally activate more neurons in that circuitry. In fact, this method of how well we can sense our own heartbeat has become a standard way to measure self-awareness.

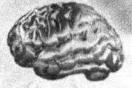

Another example of self-awareness is how we experience gut feelings or intuition. These signals originate from the insula and whilst they are by no means foolproof, the better we can read them, the more reliable our intuition.

A survey was carried out by a group of British researchers with 118 professional traders and ten senior managers at four City of London investment banks. The most successful traders (whose annual income averaged £500,000) were neither the ones who relied entirely on analytics nor the ones who just went with their gut instincts. According to the analysis, they focused on a full range of emotions, which they used to judge the value of their intuition. When they suffered losses, they acknowledged their anxiety, became more cautious, and sensibly took fewer risks. The least successful traders (whose income averaged only £100,000) tended to ignore their anxiety and keep going with their gut instincts. As a result, because they failed to heed a wider array of internal signals, they were misled and ended up in deeper trouble.

Zeroing in on sensory impressions of ourselves in the moment is one major element of self-awareness. However, more critical to leadership is the method of combining our experiences across time into a coherent view of our actual or true selves.

To be your true self means being the same person to others as you are to yourself. To some extent this means paying attention to what others think of you, particularly people whose opinions you value and who you can trust to provide honest feedback. Open awareness is useful here, where we have a broad vision of what's going on around us without getting caught up in too much detail. In this mode we simply perceive without making judgements.

This can be a little difficult for leaders who are more used to giving advice than receiving it!

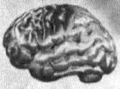

The other difficulty is that sometimes, even if you are open to input, you might not always get it, and this becomes more apparent the higher up the corporate ladder you climb.

Self-Control

"Cognitive control" is the scientific term for putting your attention where you want it and keeping it there even against the temptation to wander. This focus is one aspect of the brain's executive function, which is located in the prefrontal cortex. A colloquial term for it is "willpower" but really it's a developed resistance to distraction. Cognitive control is what executives need in order to pursue a goal despite distractions and setbacks. Managing unruly emotions is by the same part of the brain's circuitry

Focusing on Others

An Executive who can effectively focus on others usually stands out as the one who will find common ground, whose opinions carry the most weight, and with whom other people want to work. They normally emerge as natural leaders regardless of organisational or social rank.

Empathy

When we think of empathy we tend to think of a single attribute, but actually it's easy to identify three different types as follows, all important contributing factors to the success of an executive:

- emotional empathy—feeling what someone else feels;

- cognitive empathy—understanding things from someone else's perspective;

- empathic concern—sensing what someone needs from you.

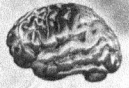

Cognitive empathy enables leaders to explain themselves in meaningful ways, a skill essential to getting the best performance from their direct reports. Contrary to what you might expect, exercising cognitive empathy requires leaders to think about feelings rather than to feel them directly.

What's more, some lab research suggests that the appropriate application of empathic concern is critical in making moral judgments. Brain scans have revealed that when volunteers listen to tales of people subjected to physical pain, their own brain centres for experiencing such pain light up instantly. But if the story they hear is about psychological suffering, the higher brain centres involved in empathic concern and compassion take longer to activate. Some time is needed to grasp the psychological and moral dimensions of a situation. The more distracted we are, the less we can cultivate the subtler forms of empathy and compassion.

Building Relationships

Generally speaking, people who lack social sensitivity are easily identified as the clueless among us. For example, a CFO who is technically brilliant but manages people by bullying or isolating them, or showing favouritism, but when confronted will shift the blame, get angry, or think that *you're* the problem. This is not usually a deliberate action – he or she is simply unaware of their shortcomings.

Social sensitivity appears to be related to cognitive empathy. Cognitively empathic executives usually excel at overseas assignments, probably because they quickly pick up implicit norms and learn the unique mental models and etiquette of a new culture. Attention to social context lets us act with skill no matter what the situation, instinctively fit in and put others at ease.

Circuitry that converges on the anterior hippocampus reads social context and leads us intuitively to behave differently with our friends than with our families or our work colleagues. In parallel with the

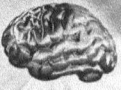

deliberative prefrontal cortex, it squelches the impulse to do something inappropriate or embarrassing.

We will address most of the above issues later in this book as part of our Neuro-Training, but hopefully this chapter has given you an oversight into how our brains control our behaviour and a hint at how you might be able to improve the way you control those functions and use them to your advantage in your position as CEO or senior manager.

Chapter 2

WHAT'S TRUE REALLY?

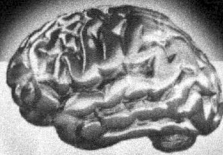

Chapter 2

WHAT'S TRUE REALLY?

> "If you want to awaken all of humanity,
> then awaken all of yourself.
>
> If you want to eliminate the suffering in the world,
> then eliminate all that is dark and negative in yourself.
>
> Truly, the greatest gift you have to give is that of
> your own self-transformation."
>
> Lao Tzu

After years of working and researching the way people operate I have noticed many similarities between them, and reduced their patterns into a single although multifaceted graphical model I call the Model of Universal Principles (MUP).

Through the use of consistent feedback regarding the adaptive abilities clients did or didn't have, I saw that people work in reproducible patterns of behaviour. And what we think we are doing consciously is only a small part of what is actually happening in the subconscious. Being privy to that subconscious activity is as much a pleasure as it is challenging.

This duality of human activity is all around us and challenging what we think we believe all the time. We call it dichotomy, paranoia, stress, 'losing it', or a myriad of other relevant terms. With further investigation we find it is really based on a triad of references buried in the subconscious and brain's architecture.

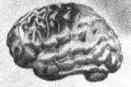

We have taken what seems to be quite a shallow look at the brain and the subconscious connections within it. Time has revealed that these connections are intricately more adaptable than we could have ever thought. These pathways of life, created within the walls of our minds, form the matrix in which the brain bathes, and is moved to create further actions in response. It is an evolving masterpiece of creativity through association and repetition.

The repetitiveness of the brain is a feature of how it tests itself. Through continually repeating the same activity the brain becomes stronger along the pathways it has decided to create. In doing so it strengthens some pathways and incorporates them into the mainstream or it goes about creating new pathways as an adaptive strategy for being prepared at any cost.

These pathways are not just random events that fill the space in our heads. They follow a greater set of relationships that take their cue from universal truths. These have been mapped out and formulated into the MUP. This model is such an eye opener when you consider that every relationship we could or have embarked upon is represented in some way within this model. And it can show us relationships within us we never knew about until now.

Let me explain it in as simple terms as I can here for sake of space and time. (That was a pun as you'll see later). By the way, we are going to talk for now about your Survival Code, which we will come back to later on in the book as part of your Neuro-Training, but for now, it's important to understand what the 'Survival Code' is.

Your Survival Code

Most of your time is taken up consciously with everyday things which must be done. You are distracted constantly away from those things you

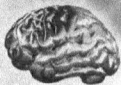

are good at and the things that would change your lives into the success you want it to be. You are overrun with conscious input, most of which you will try to block out anyway.

So the subconscious has the job of collecting all the things you don't want to know about consciously and process it into some form of usable information. To do this the subconscious categorises all the input you experience (even if you are not consciously aware of it) and attempts to use it where it can and store it where it can't. The subconscious can be acting on information you are not consciously aware of. In fact, it does this most of the time.

The more you use the subconscious this way, the more you invite its other activities to become stronger as well. You mostly do not know what they are either, so how much of your life is the way you consciously want it to be?

Pay attention! This is critical information for you to understand your life!

There are some things you have to know about the subconscious!

- The subconscious runs most of what you do.

- It pays close attention to what the genes are telling it.

- It must survive and reproduce.

- It always does the best it can to help you be better.

- It can only use what it has not what you wish you had.

- If you don't tell it what you want in the way it understands it will use what it has.

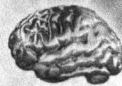

- It is literal and tries to make everything simple.

- It will take action before you even know there is a problem.

The most important of these for the discussion now is that the subconscious must survive, because it wants you to survive. You die, it dies. For it to survive it has created what I call a 'Survival Code'. This is a mixture of genetic references and the learned behaviours you develop through your life events and experience.

I can hear you say, "It's good to survive isn't it?" and the answer is: "You have already survived; you can stop doing that and do now what your survival was preparing you for – Living!!!" Too much of your life is spent on surviving at a subconscious level while life and the things you want slip away from you without even noticing till it's too late.

The Survival Code is like having two full-time jobs. One is to survive and mobilise all the resources needed to make that survival successful. At the same time you have a life to lead with its own demands and pressures. If you had two full time jobs, you would be dead in a week. Yet, in fact, we all have two jobs to do and some people will tell you they feel they have more than two.

The big challenge is, while you are doing survival, you cannot do many other things. The resources you use up 'surviving' are no longer available for the other things you want in life.

Why is it a Code?

The subconscious has formed a 'recipe' of all the main components of the events that were threatening to us at some time in life. The more threatening the event, the more components of that experience get put into a library of 'Survival Facts'.

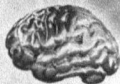

You have different 'Facts' to know when you are under threat. The problem is, you don't know consciously which are 'survival facts' and which are memories. You could start remembering some event and end up getting really stressed from just remembering a threatening event. The event is not here and now but your subconscious starts to react to it as if it is. Your resources are mobilised to survive the threat via a genetic based reaction called the Fight–Flight–Faint response. This is how you survive using your own experience as a base.

The command to survive is a standing (ongoing) order from the genes. While you are doing Flight–Fight–Faint you are preoccupied and cannot put 100% attention to what you want to be doing.

The Survival Code guarantees you will focus on survival regardless of anything else you are doing or want to do. Even this by itself is still something you can overcome, but when you make this genetic based survival response a Habit, you lose the game!

Everyone has different code content but they are all built the same way by their genes. The genetic information is at the base of the code, so you need to rewrite the code in a way the subconscious thinks comes from the genes.

You have some cool options to rewrite that content. It is a mixture of a genetic based reaction to threat and the information you have accumulated over time to build up your 'Facts' of survival. Rewrite the code and you can set yourself free. You rewrite the code by changing your neurological reactions to stress while consciously directing your attention to 'Changing the Facts'.

One of the assumptions you make about any 'Fact' is that it is real and unchangeable. In neurological terms that is untrue. You can replace or associate new Facts with any life experience. It then becomes crucial

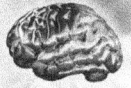

for the change process to be accepted, that the way you make the new associations must be recognisable by the subconscious as a valid genetic process. You can make the change a valid genetic process, which I will show you how to do in this book.

The Facts are usually life events that you did not like or that were not good for your natural development. For example, when a young baby is taken away from its mother, it will become more and more distressed until its subconscious tells it "You could die". The fact of being separated becomes a basis for survival.

Your Greatest Ally – The Nervous System

The Nervous System has connections to every part of who you are and can respond to any stimulus. It constantly monitors changes and is connected to systems that can be used to read those changes. It can be used as a feedback tool to know when you are heading in the right direction with the change process and indicate when a change of action is needed. It's like having a spy inside the subconscious that will tell you information if you push the right button.

To rewrite the Survival Code using the Nervous System to monitor the process, you have to also look at the Brain. The Brain is a mixture of Nervous System, Mind and Genetics all in one integrated package. If someone gave you one hundred million neurons and said, "Here you, go design a Brain," what would you do? You certainly could not reproduce what you use now and even scientists, who make it their job to know how it works, still don't understand everything it can do.

But your subconscious does!

The brain is made of various divisions that seem to compete for the 'user rights' to lots of different types of information. It is alive and, not unlike

a muscle, in that if you don't use it, some of its functions are sacrificed so the activity you are practicing can become stronger.

The two sides of the brain even have learned to develop certain functions different to each other. They attempt to coordinate as much as possible, but when the Survival Code is activated only the left hemisphere initiates actions. Some parts of the brain are activated to help the survival take place while other parts are inhibited, either so they can't interfere or it is not economical to have them running when survival seems more important.

There is a very specific action the brain takes when the Survival Code is activated. Firstly, it slows down the 'Corpus Callosum', the connecting bridge between the two hemispheres by changing the chemistry of the area. Secondly, it shuts down other 'unwanted' activities; and thirdly it preserves energy for the survival rather than thinking or planning.

Let's face it, if you are about to be eaten by a dinosaur you don't need the part of the brain required for 'future planning' to take over and create a conversation with the animal to convince it that maybe eating you isn't such a good idea in the long-term. A lot of blood is mobilised into the muscles of your body to fight or flight, while some parts of the brain remain empty and yet other parts are needed to control the fight flight process.

Even though this is an ancient survival action it has been evolved to be the most efficient. So when you see the dinosaur you immediately activate the Survival Code, which sets in place a series of neurological events that try to keep you alive. It's pretty easy to see how surviving a dinosaur attack could be necessary, but what about all the other possibilities? Some are inherited because of the nature of the evolution of the survival mechanism, but most are collected experiences that you have been through and that your nervous system has learned about.

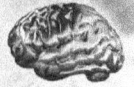

These learned 'Facts' are stored in your 'Survival Code' and used to alert the Fight–Flight mechanism to activate. The code is unique to each individual and yet uses the same genetic responses to act out its primary need – survival.

What if there is a 'Fact' in your code that says 'taxation'. Then anything you associate with taxation can start up the Survival Code and your subconscious immediately goes into survival mode. The dinosaur you could run from or fight but what do you do with a letter from the taxation dept. Do you fight it? Run from it? Pretend it's not there (the modern version of 'faint'). None of these options make the threat go away.

So now you have a survival mechanism in action but no way for it to be effective. Therefore, less chance to turn it off again. Usually the survival mechanism will reset after a good fight or run and the hormones and blood changes that take place during the survival activity are put back ready to survive the next threat.

It could be worse!

Another thing to consider is that if the mechanism is not reset, it becomes a constant action that is never turned off. This means that you are on alert all the time for ANYTHING that may be associated with any type of threat. Now the subconscious is constantly looking for what the threat may be, because its Survival Code is still activated. Anything can now become the focus of survival response. The effect of this is commonly seen as 'stresses'. Even just asking someone how they are today out of courtesy, may be met with an angry response.

Stress reactions are a signal that your Survival Code is active and needs to be reset. Until it's reset, you will continue to be stressed and reactive. If allowed to continue, this situation can and will create more problems than need to be there.

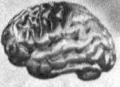

The solution is inside you

The subconscious is so adaptable that you can use it to tell you what it needs via the nervous system. By using the systems connected to the Nervous System you can find ways of associating new and better options to what the subconscious thinks it knows. Adding new information into the subconscious this way means you have control over what you rewrite, and the process of how you do it ensures the subconscious sees it as important as the old 'Code'. That means you can reset the code and, even better, rewrite its content so that no further stress reactions take place unless your life really is threatened.

By doing this, the brain can maintain many of the functions that would otherwise be turned off and use them to create new options to what before seemed like an impossible situation. These parts of the brain are needed to input new information into the Survival Code to eliminate unnecessary information that has found its way into the Code. It's like being able to do a spring clean of the subconscious so it can focus on what you want rather on what you don't want.

Habits and why you need to control them

Habits have triggers and these triggers activate a chain of events that can happen extremely quickly. As soon as your subconscious recognises any sign that a threat is about to happen, you automatically go into a stress reaction, often before you even see it yourself.

The next factor to consider in how you create and maintain your stress reactions is that the brain learns by association. You learn by creating sensory input of the environment and adding this into the current thought processes and associate them together. Usually, in a normally functioning brain, you can decide what information to keep and what to reject. This is the job of the Reticular Activating System, one of a

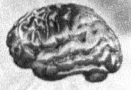

number of crucial brain functions you need to be mentally healthy and one we looked at in Chapter 1 – your gatekeeper or PA which filters out the information entering your brain.

While you are in a 'stress state', the functions of your brain are compromised and do not work efficiently. So you have incomplete processing, because the stress reactions become associated with sensory information coming in from the environment around and within you. The end result is you have a mixed jumble of information which does not make any sense. You don't know to question the perceptual processes and so do not think that what you think may be wrong. So to justify the confusion you experience from this situation you blame others around you or the memories of those in the past as the cause of your stress.

Stress is formed as a response to the outside needs/demands when we feel we don't have the resources needed.

It is easy for you to perceive that the 'trouble' comes from the outside world. The real cause of the reaction is a combination of survival mechanisms that have gained unnatural dominance over the nervous system responses in the brain.

I didn't know this when I was young. I just had to 'tuff it out', as I thought, to get accepted or recognised or both from everyone, from my parents to the other kids at school. I hated rejection to the point where I would do almost anything anyone wanted me to do so they wouldn't reject me. They did anyway which only added to my confusion and uncertainty about myself.

My self-esteem was almost nil. I did something that still has its affects today and this is the third part of the stress progression.

- First you have to fight.

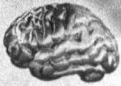

- But when that seems too insurmountable or just plain suicide, you go into flight. You realise you just have to get out of there and run like hell before you really get slammed, or worse.

- And here is the third and the real cruncher for most people. When what you are fighting is coming from inside, you can't fight it and you can't run away from it because you take it with you wherever you go. You created a perception you think is real.

That's why I like the definition of fear as 'False Evidence Appearing Real'. I don't know where that originated, but its spot on for accuracy. We all have a way of processing the internal perceptions and don't ever realise that they are not the reality 'out there' but a construct from what is already 'in here'.

When you realise that the constructions inside your mind are your personal reality and that you can change them, you will always think the stress resolution is to fight and flight or, the third 'modern' option, forget. Forgetting is a great option for the internally created stress reactions because it means you just don't allow ourselves access to those realities. Easy isn't it?

You just forget that there is a stress and you say, "It will take care of itself", and walk off to do something else. Even though you are forgetting the stress, you are still making the same reactions to the challenges you have, the internal and external ones – you have just disassociated your awareness to them.

For me, and for most people, this became one of the worst habits on the planet. This will creep over into other areas of your life. You'll start to forget where you put things, what you were going to say. Don't even talk about remembering other people's names. No way. So it is not only embarrassing but also very dysfunctional. Without a good memory you

will never be efficient at anything, without really good external supports and coping strategies.

This is one reason people think organising will help them to be less stressed. It actually takes up more of your time and you have less time to go after the real issues. Well, that's for another book, back to stress habits.

Habits have to be reorganised from the inside out.

You make your habits inside your nervous system while you consciously pay little, if any, attention to them. Yet they are the things that keep your life moving forward. Without your habits you would be totally dysfunctional because you would have to be learning everything you know all over again every day.

There is a part of you that is creating the habits as a way of helping you to be more functional and not spending so much time on remembering what you already know. This allows you to learn new stuff without losing what you already know. But this 'part' is indiscriminate when it comes to what it turns into a habit. It will turn anything into a habit just because you do something more than seven times. That's the magic number. You do anything seven or more times and you have created a neurological 'pathway' for that event or function. This may weaken if not used regularly or strengthen if you do use it often.

The process that makes the bad habits is the same process that can create New GOOD habits and you can control that consciously. I believe that if people understood this alone, they could change their life considerably. But while you are in 'forget mode' you would never think of making new habits, would you?

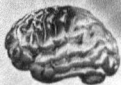

Habits are connected to each other.

You don't just have a few habits, you build them to fit into a larger pattern of behaviour where they can gain greater value by being a part of the greater whole. This is why, if you were to make a list of your habits, then ask your closest friend (and remember they are your friend) to make a list of your habits, their list would be three times longer than yours. The extent of your habitual behaviour is often surprising. And even more surprising that we don't even recognise them.

It is possible to change your life just through making the right or appropriate habits to support what you want to achieve. Steven Covey's book *The 7 Habits of Successful People* became a bestseller because it states the obvious. Without the right habits, you can't do what you want nor have the success you want either.

Let's look at this from another angle.

- Habits are being created all the time.

- The habits most activated become the strongest.

- Good habits lead to good results.

- Bad habits lead to bad results.

- Stress is usually nine parts habit.

When the habit of stress is gone you can decide what type of life experience you want to have by making a choice.

- Best of all, you can create your own best habits.

If you want to find a habit that will support your life the way you want, find someone who will teach you the right information. But just having the right information is never going to change anything. It's how much of that information you can put into practice while engaging the subconscious preferences.

As great as a new habit is for changing the direction of stress it's not the only answer. In fact, it's a small part of the answer because the subconscious forgets nothing. You may limit your access to that information but the subconscious remembers everything that ever happened to you. It remembers, using a marvellous process that is way too complicated to explain completely here but I will give you a simplified version.

Remember to remember the good stuff!

Everything our subconscious experiences, is recorded as a set of connections that make a pattern in the brain's nervous system. When you remember something the same old pattern of connections is activated and you 'experience' all that is associated to that group of connections.

Now, it's pretty silly to say that memory is just a group of connections but the nervous system is so complex that a single memory may be attached to millions of bits of information. In fact, every time you remember something, you recreate that set of connections. So this new set may now be connecting new or current values structures that you did not have when the original event was taking place.

This is a very big and important subject for understanding how your mind reveals things to you. The problem is that you alter the memory patterns often enough and change the memory to suit ourselves at any given time and think that the memory is the same and true.

How many times have you been reminiscing with a friend to find that they have a totally different memory of what you thought was the truth?

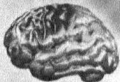

Do this little exercise and you will see what I mean.

1. Think of a memory, anything but not too traumatic, just some simple memory.

2. Close your eyes and get a clear picture in your mind as to what that memory was all about.

3. Start changing the memory perception by making it blurry and indistinct. Notice how that changes how you feel about the memory.

4. Bring the memory back to its original form.

5. Now make the perception far away as if it is shrinking as you look at it. Notice how that makes you feel differently about the memory.

6. Now consciously decide to remember something you forgot about that memory. It could be something someone said, or a colour or an event. Notice what that makes you feel about that memory.

7. Bring it back to its original for again.

The point of this is to show you that not only can you remember things about a memory that were not in your awareness the first time, but the changing of a memory can influence how you feel about the event as well. For better or worse, depending on what is associated in your mind to the change you make.

Personally important self-defining memories are the smallest unit of your life story, which begin to emerge in adolescence. The content and the associated emotional responses of those memories can even predict a person's degree of subjective distress.

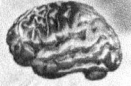

From studies they have found that good memories have vivid positive emotional responses attached to them, whilst negative memories have positive emotional responses but less vivid, while the experiences that have no positive memories attached are not remembered at all.

If you have a 'purely' negative experience with no positive emotions attached, you have far greater chance of not even remembering it at all. This is because of the third step in the stress reaction of 'Forgetting' the event even happened.

But it did happen and our subconscious is ready for it to happen again. It is now prepared for it and will react to anything that even looks remotely similar to the original event. It doesn't matter if you remember it or not for there to be a reaction to it. Interesting circumstance isn't it?

What to do is to have a way of changing those inaccessible memories even if you don't consciously remember what happened to form them in the first place.

In summary, what you don't remember has the most negative emotional responses attached to it. You need to add some positive responses to them to make them accessible so you can then change how your nervous system responds to those memories. What you remember is mostly not really causing a stress reaction and therefore is not usually what needs to be changed for stress relief or elimination.

So, we've looked at how habits can control our lives and cause us unnecessary stress, and we will look further at how to change our habits as part of our Neuro-Training later on in this book.

Chapter 3

YOU ARE A LIVING PLACEBO

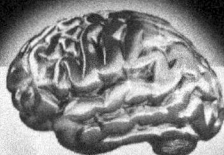

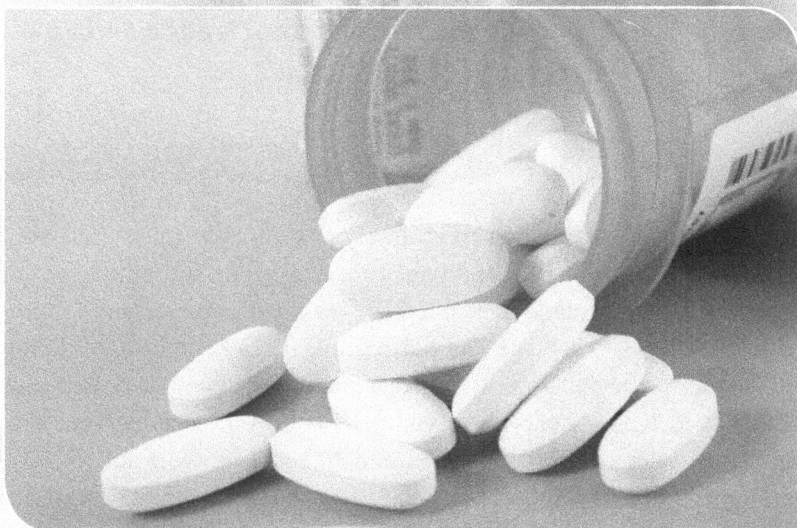

Chapter 3

YOU ARE A LIVING PLACEBO

> "I have just three things to teach:
> Simplicity
> Patience
> Compassion
>
> These three are your greatest treasures."
>
> *Lao Tzu*

> "The self-fulfilling effects of response expectancies, in which the belief that one will feel different leads a person to actually feel different."
>
> Irving Kirsch

If you have read this far, then most likely you already know that you have the entrepreneurial spirit and you are willing to do something about it. It might not always have been the case, as most entrepreneurs don't start out knowing they are one and don't think about becoming or being an entrepreneur, they just want to get something done, fast! Perhaps you, like most, haven't classified yourself as an entrepreneur but are simply drawn to building a business and life for yourself and family and are getting busy with that. Perhaps you are already the CEO of an organisation or a senior manager or owner of your own business. Either way, this information applies to you.

There are some basic definitions of what makes an entrepreneur, but for now I want you to realise that an entrepreneur doesn't think about 'why', or about 'how'! In fact, they don't even do what they do for the money! (Ooh that's hard to swallow)

Something interesting happens on the way through. Our friends at Wikipedia have this to say on the Placebo Effect. "The placebo effect is related to the perceptions and expectations of the person; if a substance is viewed by them as helpful, it can heal, but, if it is viewed as harmful, it can cause negative effects, which is known as the nocebo effect, (Latin for "I shall harm")."

In 1985, Irving Kirsch hypothesised that placebo effects are produced **by the self-fulfilling effects of response expectancies**, in which **the belief that one will feel different** leads a person to actually feel different.

*Kirsch I (1985). "Response expectancy as a determinant of experience and behaviour". American Psychologist **40** (11): 1189–1202. doi:10.1037/0003-066X.40.11.1189.*

According to this theory, the belief that one has received an active treatment can produce the subjective changes. Placebos can act similarly through conditioning wherein a placebo and an actual stimulus are used simultaneously until the placebo is associated with the effect from the actual stimulus. Both conditioning and expectations play a role in placebo effect. Conditioning has a longer-lasting effect, and can have an effect on the earlier stages of information processing. Those that think that a treatment will work display a stronger placebo effect than those that do not….

Because placebos are **dependent upon perception and expectation**, various factors that change the perception can increase the magnitude of the placebo response. For example, studies have found that the colour and size of the placebo pill makes a difference, with "hot-coloured" pills

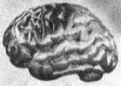

working better as stimulants while "cool-coloured" pills work better as depressants. Capsules rather than tablets seem to be more effective, and size can make a difference. One researcher has found that big pills increase the effect while another has argued that the effect is dependent upon cultural background.

It may sound a bit far-fetched but let's think about you as a placebo. Yes let's pretend you are the effect and your expectation that the effect will be positive is something you can consciously construct. Why not? If we can learn how to imagine we are a placebo instead of it happening under only specific circumstances, we could add some amazing results to our bottom line. Be able to challenge greater things with a knowing it will work and in the way we decide.

They do, though, think in a different mental construct that **creates a change of perception and expectation.** As a consequence, you, as an entrepreneur, fit the definition of placebo. **You are your own placebo so use it. If you change your perception of yourself into a positive expectation, you will get more positive outcomes. The 'nocebo' works just as well but to produce negative effects.**

That's true, being an entrepreneur is for the feeling of 'self-satisfaction of overcoming a self-made challenge'. It's a proving of yourself to yourself process! Why? So you can feel good! Fulfilment or being rich or powerful are just landmarks along the way. Accidents if you like. You'll use the 'increase of revenue and higher profitability' as yardsticks for measuring the process, but you are one of the true inventors in this world and without you we all would be in a very dangerous position.

Unfortunately, we are in a social environment that demands a certain type of thinking, and the entrepreneur has adapted to this situation to find the way to be satisfied with his/her own abilities. This has led a lot of them to believe things about themselves that are just not true.

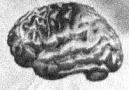

Anyway, the neurological processing that an entrepreneur goes through is the point of this discussion. They think in systems, strategies and processes that ultimately are automated. This is a direct reflection of how our body works too. Because of this parallel, the entrepreneur is a great example of how we can learn to take advantage of our resources and achieve anything we decide to.

What does an entrepreneur do within the business model?

They never stay with the 'status quo' and are always thinking of new ways to skin that cat – and they find them too. They are always exercising one hugely important quality, **Challenge to overcome RISK!** They either love it or pay no attention to it but are mindful of all the consequences of their actions. If they are wrong in the smallest of areas, they will fail and then work even harder to find out how to not do it again.

It is RISK that drives them and they derive this from attacking and overcoming challenges. If the challenges are not there, they create them.

Our nervous systems are the same, and are developed by overcoming challenges. The entrepreneur is a person who has had an experience in life that triggered a reaction to need to succeed. A need to feel that they and they alone have done everything they could to feel satisfied with their efforts.

Our nervous system is exactly the same!!!

It runs multiple systems on automatic all day and night plus, to the best of its ability, it regulates the variables within those systems to be congruent.

Just like an entrepreneur has to find the right challenge and therefore the right resources, our nervous system has to have the resources to maintain

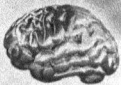

what it has to do. If the systems can be integrated and with the right resources available, our nervous systems will overcome any challenge.

Part of my job in developing Neuro-Training has been to observe people and how they operate from the inside out. I have repeatedly seen people who were failing consistently to overcome the odds with the integration of INTERNAL resources or with the addition of resources that could become internalised.

If you want to be successful, just like any other successful entrepreneur, you must find the right challenges for yourself to overcome as well as the right challenges for your business to overcome.

In Neuro-Training we have found neurological, scientifically based processes to integrate the internal systems to operate as a single working unit instead of many different competing forces that drain resources.

Consequence?

Firstly, Change your mental attitude towards RISK and express the resultant change into 'enterprise' (of any type, that's your choice).

Secondly, Find and engage in the right challenges for you as a person and your business.

Thirdly, Find and integrate the right resources to support your enterprise. The result will always be success.

You must always Risk Success! It's the best thing you can do to grow in life.

Neuro-Training can coach you into how to do the integration work, while you make the choices on where that integration will take place, and we

will come to that as we go through this book and during the exercises at the end. If you fail consistently to change, engage and integrate you will become depressed and not know it.

What is CEO Depression Syndrome (CDS) and what are the indicators?

Apparently, many successful CEOs and Entrepreneurs have bipolar disorder (manic depression). In fact, this phenomenon is so common that many business writers and bloggers refer to it as "CEO's disease" or CEO Depression Syndrome (CDS). The idea that our brightest CEOs and entrepreneurs could be susceptible to depression begs the question; how have they managed to accomplish so much?

Perhaps if you are already an accomplished CEO you will understand this and recognise the symptoms already, but for many this will be 'breaking news' and so in the following section we will look at the symptoms of CDS and how Neuro-Training can help live with them and support you if indeed you need it. Anyhow, much of CDS is stress related and that is something that definitely affects senior managers and CEOs at some point.

An article by Richard Elsberry says that bipolar disorder was common among some of the most creative people in history including: Ernest Hemingway, Leo Tolstoy, Virginia Woolf, Mark Twain, Paul Gauguin, George Handel, Gustav Mahler, Cole Porter, and Winston Churchill. Other articles claim that Steve Jobs, Ted Turner, Bill Liechtenstein, and all three founders of Netscape show signs of, or were properly diagnosed with, bipolar disorder.

Some leading experts have suggested that bipolar disorder helps people run successful companies because, "in their highest moments they dare to dream, and in their lowest moments they confront the most bleak and problematic parts of the company, instead of avoiding them".

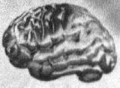

But let's be clear here, while bipolar disorder might occasionally help business people reach great heights, left unchecked it can also lead to wild, damaging behaviour, with devastating consequences for a sufferer and his or her family, friends, partners, employees – even a sufferer's entire company. According to statistics, about one in six untreated manic depressives commit suicide; even with treatment, the mortality rate is 10%. Up to the time they reach that point, however, they are often among the most celebrated and envied people in business.

Let's look at some common symptoms of depression which you may not have even thought about:

1. **You're in pain.**

   Depression and pain share some of the same biological pathways and neurotransmitters. Research has shown that about 75% of people with depression suffer recurring or chronic pain. In a Canadian study published in the journal *Pain*, people with depression were four times more likely to have intense or disabling neck and low back pain than those who were not depressed.

2. **Where did that extra roll come from?**

   Maybe from all the frozen dinners you've been eating because you don't feel like shopping or cooking? Although comfort food can raise levels of the mood-boosting brain chemical serotonin, over time emotional eating can lead to weight gain and feelings of guilt and shame, plus it does nothing to treat the underlying causes of depression.

3. **You have a short fuse.**

   If the slightest mishap sends you into a rage, or grouchy is your new normal, you may be depressed. In a 2013 study published in the

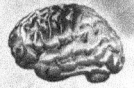

journal *JAMA Psychiatry*, 54% of people with depression reported feeling hostile, grumpy, argumentative, foul-tempered, or angry.

4. **You feel nothing.**

Feeling nothing, neutral or numb? Most of us have motivations that get us out of bed in the morning, whether it's work, exercise, socialising, or making breakfast, but for people who are depressed, those pulls dry up and things that once brought tears or smiles now barely register. This kind of behaviour is a hallmark sign of depression, and it can make you seem cold, distant or aloof, pushing away the people who would otherwise give you support and that includes your colleagues and employees.

5. **Your evening cocktail is now 3pm.**

If you're having several glasses of alcohol every night, it's probably more than a rough day at work. Nearly one-third of people with depression also have an alcohol problem, research shows. And though one drink can take the edge off, a second or third can amplify negative emotions and signs of depression—anger, aggressiveness, anxiety, and greater depression.

6. **You're glued to Facebook... or other distracting media.**

Or gambling or shopping or porn... basically, doing anything in excess, especially online compulsively and having more virtual social interactions than real ones may be a signal of depression. This might not apply if you are a CEO or Director of a busy company, but it may be apparent in your concentration levels when working alone.

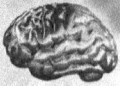

7. **Your head is in the clouds.**

   Excessive daydreaming is another sign of potential depression, relating to lack of concentration or motivation. Psychologists from Harvard University have shown that we're happiest when our minds are firmly rooted in the present moment, and when our minds wander, it can make us wistful, anxious, and unhappy.

8. **You can't make up your mind.**

   We make upwards of 70 conscious decisions every day, most of them simple, but when we're depressed, those cognitive processes take a big hit and even the little things we normally don't think twice about suddenly become weighty decisions, so from a senior management or CEO perspective this is quite stressful.

Anxiety and Depression are the most popular form of distress response.

They are so common that there are thousands of searches on these terms on the internet every day, all from people trying to find an answer.

It's all a matter of degree

You are depressed (read not doing what you want or doing something you don't want) and the reason why you are doing what you do changes for the worse, now you have a reason to expect the future will be no good for you. You become anxious and find you are having panic attacks and your fears become a stronger influence over your thinking.

It is not very long before you develop 'phobic' reactions. These fears have always been there but until this anxiety developed the fears were under control, naturally. With your loss of control of the fears they grow

stronger and become phobias. The difference between a fear and a phobia is that you still have some control over a fear, even if it is diminishing. In the case of a phobia, all control is lost and the phobic reaction now drives the distress response.

The effect of the stress reactions accumulates and turns into a 'distress plateau'

If you experience a major challenge (especially over an extended period of time), this plateau acts as a kind of bank or store of reactions that stops any ability to reduce the distress and keeps you 'stuck' in a continuing reaction. Post-Traumatic Stress Disorder (PTSD) is such an example. In PTSD there is only more, added distress, and all the while your ability to escape this cycle is continually diminishing.

Once you have progressed into either the phobic area or the PTSD (the library of accumulating distress), you lose control of the distress response and are now governed by people, events and circumstances around you.

At this stage it seems your only way of reducing the stress is to avoid people and avoid doing anything of responsibility, which, let's face it, isn't an option for a CEO!

Your mind now works in an ever-increasing pattern of confusion, so even the simplest of small changes sets off massive disproportionate reactions. These things can be reversed but they are just different applications of the same underlying mechanism and will have varying amounts of associated memories.

Changing the activation of this underlying mechanism will start to reduce the addition of 'new' stress and give you the opportunity to start creating some better 'supportive' habits. The habit of distress encompasses the

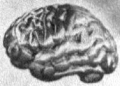

mental, emotional, physical and energetic areas of your life and, in your subconscious and nervous system, are all linked with each other.

Let me summarise with this example:

You may have an 'impression' that comes from the bad things that happened in your childhood. Let's say you had an experience with your parents, whereby when you were naughty, they beat you and put you into a dark closed room where the cockroaches and mice found you.

(Unpleasant I know, but not uncommon in some parts of the world).

All the elements of these experiences are associated together and become a big mixed bag of triggers which will reactivate that original distress at any time.

Later in life, you see a mouse or a cockroach or maybe see someone smacking their child and all the distress responses become real again. Your nervous system starts to respond just as you did in the original experience but you consciously think your response is related to the current circumstances.

This is the conflict between the two internal pathways showing.

Your behaviours will now follow the same behaviours as you had originally and the stress reactions are reinforced. But the really sad thing is, even if you make a conscious decision to change something at this time, it will be because of the distress response and have little influence in resolving the cause of the stress.

You will most likely try to create some strategy to avoid the issue arising again or to try to find a solution that sounds plausible. None of the mental decisions made at this time will be the right answer for you because they are made with the distress mentality not your clear thinking processes.

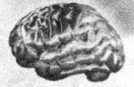

Any decisions you make while under the influence of a habitual distress response (read confusion) will deform the perspective of the decision. While you think you are making the right decision, in fact, you are making the wrong one. Then, the decisions you make are not for us but to justify having the stress reactions. All this happens in the subconscious and you are usually only aware you are stressed but never aware of the effect it is having.

This 'in-built' stress platform acts as a starting point for so many wrong decisions and inappropriate behaviours and will never serve you well in finding appropriate solutions. Anything that sounds plausible is accepted, and you never question your decisions if they seem plausible to you. Even if they are totally wrong for what you say you want.

The situation becomes increasingly worse until eventually your hormones become so out of balance that they start to 'take over' the nervous system. This will affect your mental, emotional and physical responses to life and the challenges you are confronted with.

The neurological reality is clear. While we are stressed and realise we cannot change anything now, we are depressed. This is primarily processed in the left side of our brain. While it's here the result will be a defence reaction. When we have the realisation that this will continue into the future the processing moves from the left brain (Past events) to the right brain (Future events). Now we are projecting the stress into the future along with the realisation we cannot change anything. Suddenly our future is destroyed and what do we do? Go into fear reactions we call Anxiety. Same reactions and concepts just in a different part of the brain.

You should try this exercise just because you can. Take a ball in one hand. Think of your anxiety, I mean really get anxious and start throwing the ball from one hand to the other. Keep doing this until the anxiety dissipates. Create the anxiety again and repeat throwing the ball. Do this

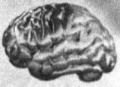

as often as you need to until you can no longer make the anxiety in the first place. You will be amazed at how fast your bipolar, PSTD, anxiety and other compulsive behaviours will just dissolve over a relatively short period of time. Don't question it, just do it. Then wonder about how it works!

A Universal Set of Relationships – The Model of Universal Principles

This Model is part of the philosophical model used in Neuro-Training as a way of identifying contexts that are in conflict and then identifying what to do about changing their relationships. What most people don't realise is the nervous system has the job of expressing and experiencing values.

If you are 'running' two sets of values at the same time and these have conflicting results, you create internal conflicts that the nervous system has to try to compensate for. It often cannot do this because of either a lack of resources or, and most commonly, you are too busy being 'stuck' in your distress to recognise any other options.

Each of the areas identified on this illustration are representative of **sets of values which, by definition, are contexts.**

It is a three-dimensional model which is unfolded in this illustration.

This model means a lot to a Neuro-Trainer and may not seem to be that relevant to you at the moment but each heading on this chart is a set of values. We can compare these 'sets' of values with your internal response to a challenge and therefore identify where there is a conflict occurring.

From there we can identify what type of association may be of benefit to that set of values and therefore allow the nervous system to take a new pathway or action based on the new value association.

Any reaction we have to anything in life will show under one or more of these contexts and gives the Neuro-Trainer a way of going straight to the cause of conflict instead of just covering it up. Even better there will always be a best way of making the necessary changes which can then easily be identified.

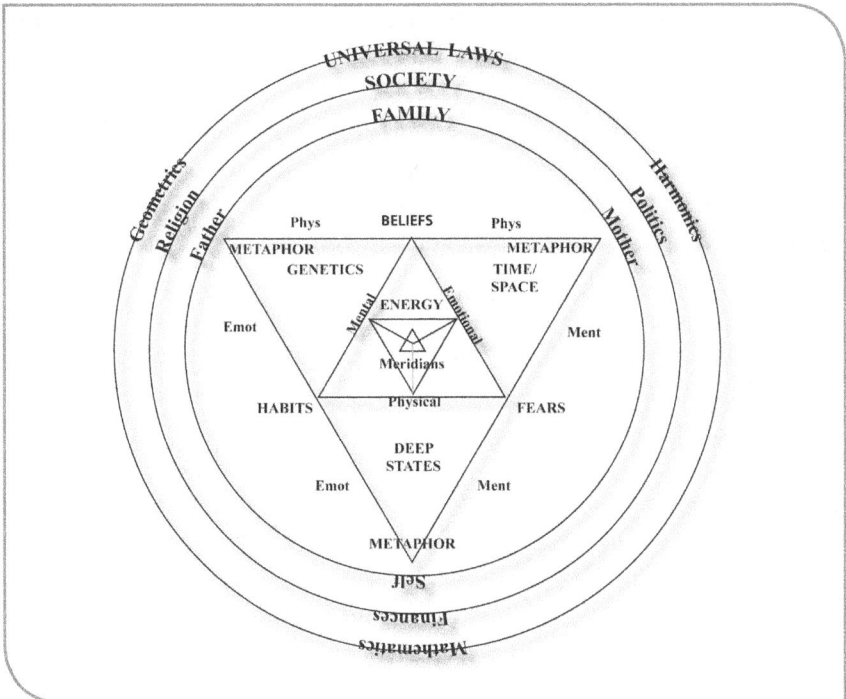

The Mental edge represents all the possible values that relate to mental processing. The Emotional edge relates to all the emotional related values and expressions, and the Physical edge relates to all the physical values and expressions.

These three contexts are part of every context and experience you could ever create in your life and as such are the three basic elements of

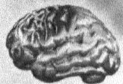

everything you do. Making sure there is no conflict between these three areas is crucial to a conflict free, and therefore, long life.

The combination of these basic elements gives rise to understanding better the relationship between Fears, Habits and Beliefs. Fears exist as a mixture of emotional responses and actions taken. The Habits are patterns (mental) acted on automatically. Beliefs are a mixture of concept (mental) and values (emotional).

All these relationships are influential in determining any response to any challenge. If these elements are in balance with each other, the decisions made will be in balance. If the relationships between them are in conflict, the decisions you make will reflect conflict and may even create more conflict.

I will not spend a great deal of time here discussing the negative effects of 'conflict', suffice it to say, that with conflict you die earlier and without it you have a greater quality of life, and more of it too.

The centre area of the triangle represents the energetic qualities that act as a communication system between all the other contexts in this model. I must say here that this is not just a product of my imagination. This has been developed over years of testing and research, using Neuro-Training, to determine the universally correct set of relationships as they relate to human behaviour.

So I can hear you saying, "What does this have to do with my business?" It's very simple really, if you want to resolve a distress response, you have to make changes in the context that the stress reaction originated in.

For example – you feel stressed at work and everyone around you is against you or your ideas, but the reason why you feel stressed originally is a misunderstanding between you and your partner.

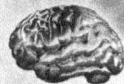

While the stress between you and your 'significant other' is unresolved, your subconscious is trying to work out a solution to that and at the same time has gone into a distress response which means you can't create new options. The end result is a process that goes around in circles and never resolves itself, unless there is new input of needed relevant information and a change from stress reaction to solution orientation.

With this process bouncing around inside your subconscious, you go off to work and expect that all will go well? Probably not, because you are subconsciously distracted from the current external requirements which they themselves start to take on the nature of the problem.

Colleagues just see you as a "grumpy old ***" or a reactive "son of a ^^^^" because they don't know the turmoil going on inside you and your nervous system.

If you attempt to resolve this in the context of work, it will not work. It is when you start to recognise that it was the emotional response to your spouse or partner that underlies the current reactions that your reactions may start to change.

Attempting to balance the work challenges with an emotional response originating at home will be unsuccessful.

Value drives you – it's the job of the nervous system

This Model has also a defining quality to it as well. It has given us a better understanding of the relationships between Mental, Emotional and Physical values also some wonderful definitions of Fear, Habits and Beliefs.

The latter occur at the 'points' of the triangle. These points are the combination of two of the basic elements and reveal another definition of Fears, Habits and Beliefs. Then 'Fear' becomes a mixture of the physical

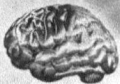

and the emotional contexts while it becomes obvious habits are a result of physical and mental combining. Beliefs are then seen as a mixture of the mental values and the emotional values.

Looking at Fears, Habits and Beliefs this way gives you some great insights into what is really happening within the values structures in your subconscious. Many people think Fear is an emotional response, yet it is actually a combination of feelings (emotional) attached to physical (physical) survival responses. It also becomes obvious that Fear has little if any mental values, expressions or control attached to it.

This means when you are in a phobic reaction there is practically no mental input into the process. The result is that when you are in fear you are brain dead. The expanded discussion on the Model of Universal Principles is for another book, but I may refer back to this basic model at times to illustrate a point.

Summary:

- Stress is a symptom that is more correctly named distress.

- It is based on a survival response that can become habitual.

- It is all to do with the expression of conflict of certain values.

- It always involves Mental or Emotional or Physical responses.

- It must always be resolved in its original context.

Another of the basics in Neuro-Training

It's actually a really interesting time in health and human sciences as we are in a great position to take advantage of the neuroscience research

and turn it into a practical reality. I feel a little sorry for the research scientists as they are stifled as to what to do with their discoveries. And I am very happy at the same time that they are stifled as it gives us a clear shot at utilising their results for the betterment of our clients.

There are five elements and six styles so there had to be some anomaly here, and it turned out to be a contextual one. The 'Styles' that relate to the Five Elements are the internally focussed processes while the sixth is an external focus process – the social intuition.

My research showed which brain parts relate to the function of the Five Elements and what to look for to determine how to utilise these styles.

Here is a summary of the Chinese Elemental qualities.

Chinese Element	Resultant Quality
Fire	Transformation
Earth	Intention
Metal	Courage
Water	Will Power
Wood	Motivation

I have categorised these **Qualities as they relate to the Control Cycle** of the Chinese Theory and they look like this:

Transformation controls Courage using Self Reflection while the aggravator is Distraction

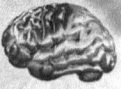

Courage controls Motivation with Balance while the aggravator is Imbalance.

Motivation controls Intention using Planning while the aggravator is Bad Habits.

Intention controls Will Power with Relative Response while the aggravator is Inconsistent Behaviour.

Will Power controls Transformation by controlling Rate of Change while the aggravator is Fear.

These strategies can be changed consciously but you have to know consciously which Quality is affecting you to be able to do that. And no single Quality is working by itself either, so it's not so easy to know where to go to make the right changes. These Qualities are related to survival and how we see ourselves processing life events. The combination of inherited patterns and learned patterns will determine which of these Qualities will dominate and which not.

Perhaps you are using one Quality for everything that happens in life? Perhaps the use of that Quality is not efficient? Perhaps while you are only using that one Quality you are stopping the natural flow of growth and development the other Qualities could afford you?

If you fall into the trap of accommodating your life to these Qualities you become subject to your ancestry as these are all inherited patterns. They are genetically based as neuroscience research has discovered.

You don't have to learn about these if you don't want to and most CEOs I have worked with are interested to know how it affects them but don't want to know any more than that. That is fine as the CEO brain is always looking for information to better its cause and eliminate the unnecessary

or limiting effects. The CEO Brain is always trying to keep it simple, keep it direct.

I have subsequently developed processes to utilise these contexts to eliminate any restrictive conditioning that may active at a subconscious level. I use these and other Five Element Characteristics with my 'Executive' clients, to ascertain where they are stuck at a subconscious operating level. I'll give you access to how this is done later in the book (if you're good that is).

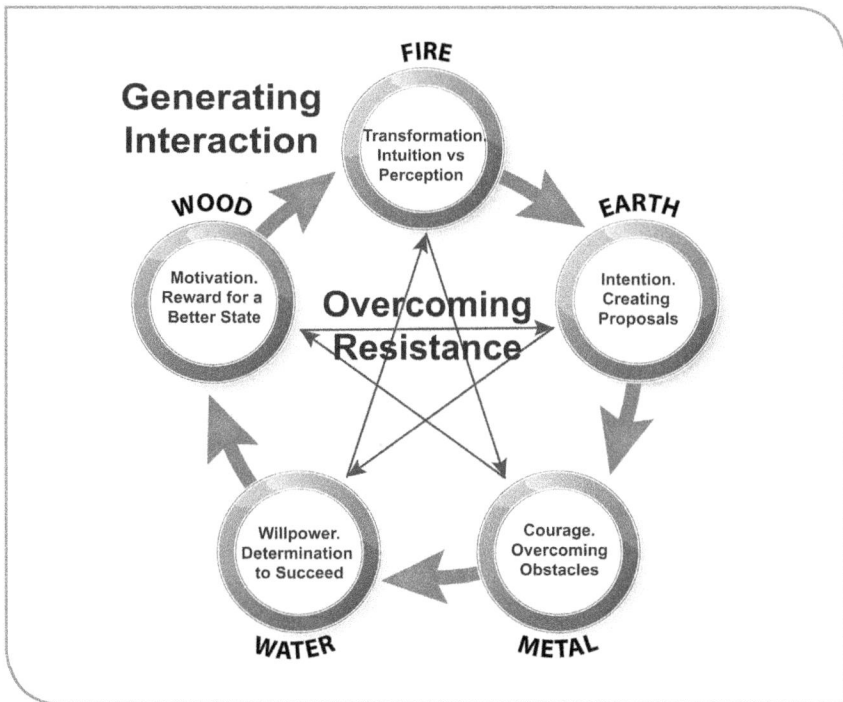

An Illustration of the Five Elements and the relationships between them.

Chapter 4

WE HAVE ALL BEEN THERE

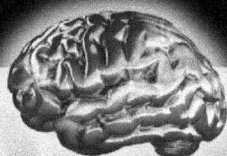

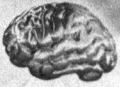

Chapter 4

WE HAVE ALL BEEN THERE

> "Emotions are related to certain activities in brain areas that direct our attention, motivate our behaviour, and determine the significance of what is going on around us."
>
> Unknown

I would like to share a personal experience. Having spent many years practicing 'Neuro-Training', I had noticed that there was something missing which I felt compelled to fix, and that was an in-cohesive and inconsistent approach to developing this into a productive and beneficial industry. I saw problems people had in utilising techniques which I already had the answers to.

The prevailing issue was a lack of structure to enable a practitioner to be efficient with their clients, which meant that any change would be an improvement. I didn't agree with this, and set about finding a structure that would support all of what was observed in using Neuro-Training.

Recognising that the use of these techniques can change a persons' life very quickly, and my background of playing many sports, gave me an instinctive understanding of kinaesthetic responses.

I have always had an inquiring mind and my discovery that these techniques could be used as tools for deeper investigation of issues inside the nervous system encouraged me to investigate further. My

findings not only surprised me, but have developed into a new modality of understanding for modifying human behaviour.

Clients and practitioners are often looking for a bigger solution than the problem actually requires, and this can lead them to being side-tracked into different 'solutions', many of which are inappropriate or inconsistent with what is really needed.

I had the investigative ability but I didn't understand how to implement it using Neuro-Training, which relies on a feedback phenomenon of changes in muscle response of the client. I found that difficult problems could be rectified, sometimes immediately. As an example, using it to help win the Australian Judo Championships, convinced me it was something I had to use. It became immediately apparent that this application could also help others as well, the evidence being how people changed and so quickly. This made me think outside the generally accepted norms and so now I focus on principles that work together rather than just techniques.

The reason why I would really like to share this new way of thinking is because of how it can bring about the types of change you want as a CEO and as a person.

I have spent over 45 years developing and researching this phenomenon, which has developed into more than a health modality; it has become a human science modality. In my early years I was just enthusiastic and curious but as I developed more techniques and then workshops, I gradually received feedback from those using the techniques which confirmed how wonderful they were as a solution for their problems.

I made it my mission to learn as much as I could about human function and how to adapt it all for positive change. What I ended up doing was learning an array of techniques that, if all used at once on a single client, would take two weeks to fully implement. Even then I wouldn't know if I'd actually done the right thing for the client.

What I did learn was that it seems where there are major challenges in our lives, major solutions are not far behind them, and I found this solution through new trainers from America who had a more liberal view on how to apply some of these techniques.

I must give credit to the person that I consider to be my first mentor, Gordon Stokes, for showing me a way of thinking about using these techniques, and for showing me that we are all human and even with our weaknesses there are still principles that we can use to help ourselves. When I think back to the time when I almost gave up and quit pursuing this completely, I thank Gordon for bringing me back to a pathway that, so far, has never ended and has created enormous benefit for those who also discover Neuro-Training.

I made a decision to integrate as many valid principles into Neuro-Training as I could find, and once I had made that decision everything became really easy to the point now where we have a diploma of Neuro-Training and people understand the principles of how it functions first, and then build the techniques into that working model.

I didn't know it when I started my research, but soon found that training is based on context as a group of values and that our brain functions according to groups of values. The conflicts we experience are from the conflict between these different groups of values.

My legacy in writing this book is to help you understand the freedom that exists in understanding how to challenge your nervous system.

A big realisation for me was that adaptive patterns and the conflict for dominance between these patterns creates the resultant decisions and answers we give ourselves, largely because they are plausible, but not because they are necessarily true or right for you.

In looking at the relationship between principles that are real and those that are not, I came to realise that if something is true it has a relationship to something else that is true. I started paying more attention to context and to the value structures my clients where showing, which revealed some remarkably consistent patterns of behaviour. These have become references and elements within our theoretical **Model of Universal Principles** (MUP).

MUP is a graphical model which shows the relationships between different contexts as a basic structure of how the subconscious works and where it doesn't. This is why I focus so much on this model in my training and in working with my CEO clients. Without this model it's very difficult to understand the pathway that the subconscious is taking at any given time and therefore almost impossible to find the right solution. You can imagine my happiness at being able to use such a map for the subconscious and for the nervous system, and for its relationship to the genetic system. It has taught me the relationship between these three main areas, and why it's so important for this work to be exposed to the people who will gain the most benefit and yield the most influence as a consequence.

We have progressed far from the idea that any change is good and we are approaching the understanding that the best change is necessary. The means we can find the best changes through the use of Neuro-Training techniques and in applying those techniques to create the greatest breakthroughs and the greatest of achievements.

This model has taught me to look at human behaviour and therefore symptoms as a contextual exercise that reveals underlying values that are in conflict. Once that conflict is removed we have a compounding effect of the immediate change in the nervous system influencing the function of the rest of the brain.

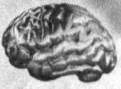

Emerging Emotions

There is a lot of attention these days on the role that emotions have in how we function. We have the decision-making process which is primarily a war between different electrical circuits in the brain that are competing to express certain values, how the brain assigns value to things and different parts of the brain assign different levels of value to those same things. This creates competition in our brain to try to find out what it is that we really want in our mind. This is primarily a mental process.

Everything depends on movement in our body and when we stop moving, it's dead. Yes, we need energy to move and we need direction. We need time and we need the ability to navigate through life, but the perceptive element itself is movement. So, we can tap into that process which produces movement and track back to find out what level the value conflict is that may be interfering with that movement. That is why we use a change of muscle response in Neuro-Training as our major feedback tool because it gives us the ability to track back to the point of value conflict. Once we have discovered that point we can use association to build in better neurological options at that point and so give the subconscious a new way of doing things.

Fortunately for us, the subconscious will always take the better option, but it can't do that if the better option is not supplied in a recognisable form. The form it recognises is neurological and we have developed Neuro-Training to be the vehicle for adding new information into the subconscious.

One of the realisations I had in developing Neuro-Training is the evolutionary effect of experience on a nervous system and our mind. This is nothing new and has been discussed in neuroscience for many decades, but because there has not been an appropriate tool for measuring

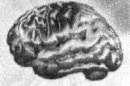

change until this time people have not realised that there is a tendency to move towards certain qualities and values that we hold deep within our being.

One of these values is competency

When the nervous system is trained to become competent, you create what I call genius neural evolution. This is where it tries to become more competent and more congruent, which gives birth to new emergent neurology. Our nervous system is constantly trying to give birth to new neural pathways as it discovers new and better ways of being competent and congruent, until the value of invincibility is achieved. I'm not saying that everybody is invincible but I am saying that the nervous system desires to become invincible and we have discovered the mechanisms of how it attempts to and how to help it do that.

Emotions

Emotions seem to be such powerful elements in human experience. No single neurological system inside us can express the same values as other neurological systems. The systems that result in our experiencing emotions are actually monitoring the interface activity between one set of systems and other sets of systems. Emotions become a feedback mechanism via the chemistry in our body, which rewards our positive learning and tries to inhibit negative experiences. There are recognisable similarities between the different systems that give us more competent and congruent adaptive patterns and there are also patterns of behaviour that lead us to negative experiences and dysfunctional results which I call compensatory patterns. We attempt to train the nervous system to recognise how effortless it is to follow adaptive patterns and so create the foundation of Adaptive Neurology. Left to our own devices we only discover those things that are of a short-term value which compromise any long-term value that we may wish for.

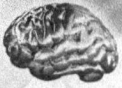

Overcoming the most appropriate challenge in your life will give you three things;

1) A new skillset;

2) More competence;

3) Immunity to the emotional associations to challenges.

The means by which we gain competence is by overcoming the most appropriate challenges, and, because we are all uniquely different in our nervous system, different people respond to different challenges in different ways. In so doing, learn different things. It still amazes me to see people doing the same things over and over and expecting different results, and understandably this has become a definition of insanity.

However, I also understand why people do this, and why they know they have a problem – and how they don't recognise that they also have the answer to that problem. The reason is that the answer is held in a different context than where they experience the problem, and so their attention and awareness can never connect the two. If their subconscious could connect them it would, and then they would not have the problem in the first place. Most people don't even realise that's what is happening inside them and then they wonder why they make the wrong decision, sometimes even when they actually know it's the wrong decision. Then we blame habits and habitual response for 'making me do it'.

Once we understand the internal functioning of the mind and how it influences the brain we can quickly recognise the brains' influence over the nervous system and then the nervous systems' influence over the muscles in the body, therefore behaviour. As a consequence, your subconscious can show us how many steps there are as a plan for achieving freedom from conditioning, from compensation, and head

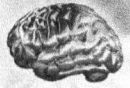

us towards financial freedom, entrepreneurial freedom and personal freedom.

Emotional Immunity

Whether you know it or not your emotions are an expression of the value structure that is associated to your mental activity as well as your physical activity. These emotions group together, creating a network of values and their expressions, which may come to the surface at any time, sometimes suddenly, sometimes we have a warning. Nevertheless, we are never given the opportunity to be taught how to utilise emotions as a value expression to our advantage.

The answer to this you will find with the Options Generator section in this book; a technique which I believe to be the most powerful way we have of associating new options to and within the nervous system. Learn how to master this technique and you will gain great influence within yourself and give yourself the ability to achieve the things you want in business and in life.

If you were to imagine that you had three wishes from a magic genie, what would be your first wish? How would that change your life if you had it? If those changes were already in your life how would that make you feel?

Let me ask you this; if you had those feelings now, would you still make the same wish or would you change it? Isn't it true that we desire those things that we think we don't have and yet when we stop denying those things to ourselves we realise we had them all along?

These are some of the questions I would typically ask my CEO clients, and then we work on establishing those emotions that they have suppressed either through fear, through suppression or through life

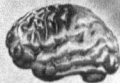

conditioning. In any case our subconscious is looking to balance the value systems we have in our genetic coding, the values we established from life experiences and the perceived values that we think we do not yet have. If life was a giant recipe and we realised that the recipe we were given isn't what we want, Neuro-Training will show you how to change that recipe to not just a better recipe but to the best recipe it can be.

When you experience overcoming similar challenges, the earlier associated emotions seem to have less influence on your decision-making and help you develop emotional immunity. That does not mean you have no emotions, it simply means you can now choose the emotions you want to experience in any given situation.

I have spoken of Competence, Challenge and Congruence and now the fourth C which is Choice. The great objective in training the nervous system is to be able to not only choose, but to also choose from the most relevant options. Choice is the ability to create more than one, two or three possibilities. Choice is three or more possibilities as options or pathways that you can follow.

You get to choose, and as a consequence you learn from the choice. The more we learn from choice the more efficient we become in our lives, in our businesses, in relationships and in our minds.

If I was to show you a way of becoming more competent by overcoming challenge through making congruent choices would you be interested in experiencing the result? I think you would, otherwise you might find yourself repeating the same patterns over and over and never getting the rewards you deserve.

As well as becoming more prolific in what you produce in your life you will develop the gravitational pull of influence that catapult you to results in your life that effect hundreds if not thousands of other people.

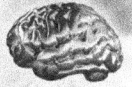

The model we use starts by focusing on you, the individual, and all of the components that make you function the way you do. It then focuses on the influence of family and how that moulds us and our behaviours for relationships with the outside world. It then continues to identify societal influence and how society values can destroy the greatest of ambitions and dehumanise the greatest potential. Finally, it helps you recognise your relationship to Universal laws and principles that can guide you into greater spheres of influence that you could never have imagined.

It's an evolutionary process that turns ordinary people into 'Kings', it turns teachers into 'Sages' and helps us to recognise that our potential is not a gift, it is a right.

Chapter 5

YOUR BRAIN IS ON YOUR SIDE, IT WILL PROVE IT TO YOU

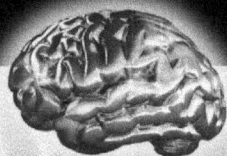

Chapter 5

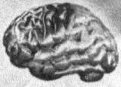

YOUR BRAIN IS ON YOUR SIDE, IT WILL PROVE IT TO YOU

"When we are no longer able to change a situation, we are challenged to change ourselves."

Viktor E Frankl

Take charge of the process of creating your own challenges FIRST, and then apply what you discover. Go for changing yourself first and with what you learn from that you have a lifetime of wisdom to draw from. Even implementing what others have learned in overcoming their challenges can be inserted into your neurology and what your brain does!

What does your brain really pay attention to?

Previous experience predicts and guides our brain to where it should pay attention. Culture also makes a difference, as you might expect, as this really affects our upbringing and consequently experiences, which in turn dictates our memories. However, whether in school or in business, these differences can greatly affect how an audience perceives a given presentation, for example. Instinctively, we don't pay attention to boring things.

We do, however, pay attention to things like emotions, threats and sex. Regardless of who you are, or what your culture might be, the brain pays a great deal of attention to these questions: Can I eat it? Will it eat me? Can I mate with it? Will it mate with me? Have I seen it before? These

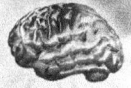

are pretty basic and instinctive reactions as you would probably expect. It's about survival.

So, if what we pay attention to is influenced by our memory, let's have a closer look at that. Most experts believe that the human brain can only hold about seven pieces of information for less than 30 seconds! Which means your brain will struggle to remember even a seven-digit phone number. However, you can improve memory, and there are plenty of tricks to help you do that. If you want to extend the 30 seconds to a few minutes or even an hour or two, you will need to consistently re-expose yourself to the information. Memories are so volatile that you have to repeat them to remember.

An example of improving your memory; many of us have trouble remembering names, especially when we are introduced to several people at once, or at a party with lots of people and lots going on. If for example you are introduced to Jane, it helps to repeat her name and also internally add more information about her such as what she is wearing and what colour or pattern. Adding more information may seem counterintuitive at first but study after study shows it improves your memory.

Most of us probably remember repeating our multiplication tables at school, and hopefully we still remember them now!

Attentional Processes

The attentional process is extremely complex and consumes lots of brain power.

An effective attentional system must be able to:

1. quickly identify and focus on the most important item in a complex environment;

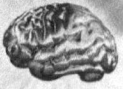

2. sustain attention on its focus while monitoring related information and ignoring other stimuli;

3. access memories that aren't currently active, but that could be relevant to the current focus;

4. shift attention quickly when important new information arrives.

Our principal attentional activity is **constant focus**. Our brain must decide what's most important in terms of context, and then focus on it while we merely monitor the context. The stupid attentional lapses and decisions we make, such as backing our car into a visible post, are a constant reminder that we have yet to achieve perfection in attending to the important and ignoring the unimportant! Emotion obviously dominates reason in many attentional decisions, and a stressful situation can chemically trigger an intense focus on something unimportant—such as when we work on an unimportant task to avoid facing a looming deadline on an important project.

As mentioned earlier, our attentional system provides us with a short-term memory buffer that allows us to hold a few units of information for several minutes while we determine whether to go on to something else or store the data in our long-term memory. The advantage of this limited capacity is that it forces us to constantly select a relatively small focus of attention from a large (and often confusing) sensory field. The disadvantage is that it contributes to our human tendency to make inappropriate snap judgments.

Measured Brain Activity

By using electroencephalography, or EEG, researchers were able to take measurements of performers' brains. This type of equipment and methodology is used by hospitals to determine possible brain injuries

after traffic accidents, but fortunately, EEG can also be used to look at the extent of integration and development of several brain processes.

The researchers looked at three different measurements that all reflect how well the brain works as a whole: 1) Coherence, which shows how well the various parts of the brain cooperate; 2) Amount of alpha waves, which reflect restful alertness; and 3) How economically or effectively the brain works.

The three measurements are combined in an expression of brain refinement, the Brain Integration Scale.

In the past, 'world-class performance', especially in respect to management, has been mostly regarded from a psychological point of view. Researchers often explain management skills as a result of special personal or psychological characteristics that some have, and others don't.

Peak Experiences and Higher Mind/Brain Development

The researchers found it's not just that their brains function differently; the world-class performers also had particular subjective experiences that were associated with their top performances – these were called peak experiences. These experiences were characterised by happiness, inner calm, maximum wakefulness, effortlessness and ease of functioning, absence of fear, transcendence of ordinary time and space, and a sense of perfection and even invincibility.

Using world-class athletes selected by the National Olympic Training Centre in Norway, the first study was carried out at the Norwegian School of Sport Sciences. The tests included screening athletes' brains using EEG and also interviewing each athlete about their experiences whilst performing at their very best. The result showed a wide range of peak experiences.

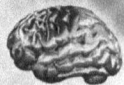

It seems that superior mind–brain development includes various aspects and parts of the brain working together in an integrated way. Among world-class performers this integration appears especially well developed.

Presenting a New Theory

As a result of this research, a new theory has been developed; a Unified Theory of Performance, which suggests that higher levels of mind–brain development form a platform for higher performance, irrespective of profession or activity.

"It seems like these mind–brain variables represent a fundamental potential for being good, really good, in the particular activity one has decided to carry out," says Dr. Harung, researcher.

Across all three recent studies there was consistency in that top-level performers outscored the control groups in a test of moral development. Higher moral development implies an expanded awareness where one is able to satisfy the interests of other people and not just their own needs. Harung found it remarkable that high levels of performance, in a wide spectrum of activities, are connected to high moral standards.

"This should give an extra push to act morally, in addition to a better self-image, fewer sleepless nights and a good reputation," Dr. Harung says. "The key to top-level performance, therefore, seems to be that we make more use of our inherent capabilities."

Implications of the Research

The discovery that brains of world-class performers have similar characteristics, raises some important questions, such as: 1) Is there a way one can develop one's brain to have more of these characteristics

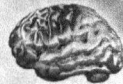

and thereby perform at a higher level?; and 2) Can measuring a person's brain predict the potential for someone to be a world-class performer?

Neuro-Training as the natural remedy.

Neuro-Training is a drug free, non-invasive way to permanently reorganise neurological difficulties and challenges within the brain itself, such as attention deficit disorder, dyslexia and other learning disorders. This cutting edge modality improves the ability to learn and retain information, removes phobias, anxiety, and is very effective at helping individuals struggling with PTSD and depression. It does use your own systems as feedback to produce automatic changes within the nervous system without drugs or synthetic interventions.

NT is an all-natural alternative therapy based on the latest neuroscience findings and uses changes of muscle response, combined with acupressure points and other reflexes to access the subconscious processes in the brain and to locate and remove conflicts. Brain Integration 'awakens' areas of the brain previously blocked by subconscious stress by rerouting the blood flow within the brain therein changing brainwave patterns. In this way we can retrain the brain's use of its resources and achieve high performance results naturally.

Why Do We Have a Brain?

You may reason that we have a brain to perceive the world or to think, and that's completely wrong. If you think about this question for any length of time, it's blindingly obvious why we have a brain. We have a brain for one reason and one reason only, and that's to produce adaptable and complex movements. Movement is the only way you have of affecting the world around you – everything goes through contractions of muscles.

Think about communication for example – speech, gestures, writing, and sign language – they're all important and mediated through contractions

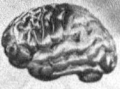

of your muscles, but they're only important to either drive or suppress future movements. There can be no evolutionary advantage to laying down memories of childhood or perceiving the colour of a rose if it doesn't affect the way you're going to move later in life.

Now for those who don't believe this argument, we have trees and grass on our planet without a brain, but the clinching evidence is the humble sea squirt. It's a rudimentary animal with a nervous system and swims around in the ocean in its juvenile life. At some point of its life, it implants on a rock, and the first thing it does, is to digest its own brain and nervous system for food. Once you don't need to move, you don't need the luxury of that brain.

Movement is the first sense ever experienced by our nervous system and the most important function of the brain. Scientific understanding of how the brain controls movement is not being handled very well, in fact, it's doing extremely poorly in this area of science.

Yet it's such an extremely important piece of the jigsaw puzzle that we really need to include it in our evaluation of behaviour and actions.

When you send a command down your arm, it causes muscles to contract. Your arm or body moves, and you get sensory feedback from vision, from skin, from muscles and so on. The trouble is these signals are not the beautiful signals you want them to be. So one thing that makes controlling movement difficult is sensory feedback is extremely noisy. Now by noise, I mean a random uncontrolled or erratic impulse that corrupts a signal.

For example, if you put your hand under a table and try to localise it with your other hand, you can be off by several centimetres due to the noise in sensory feedback. Forget about trying to hit the bull's eye in darts, just aim for the same spot over and over again. You have a huge spread of

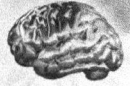

area due to movement variability. And more than that, the outside world, or task, is both ambiguous and variable. The teapot could be full, it could be empty. It changes over time. So we work in a sensory movement task soup of noise.

Neurological noise is so demanding in your nervous system that society places a huge premium on those of us who can reduce its negative consequences. If you're lucky enough to be able to knock a small white ball into a hole several hundred yards away using a long metal stick, our society will be willing to reward you with hundreds of millions of dollars.

The brain goes through a lot of effort to reduce the negative consequences of this noise and variability.

The brain is making precise predictions and subtracting them from the sensations we experience internally. Yep the brain is cancelling the sensory consequences and underestimating the force it's producing. So it re-shows, the brain makes predictions, and fundamentally changes the precepts. So we've made inferences (brain), we've done predictions (nervous system), now we have to generate actions (muscles).

But we've got a problem because tasks are symbolic – I want to drink, I want to dance – but the movement system has to contract 600 muscles in a particular sequence. And there's a big gap between the task and the movement system which is bridged in infinitely many different ways via the nervous system.

Think about just a point to point movement. I could choose these two paths out of an infinite number of paths. Having chosen a particular path, I can hold my hand on that path as infinitely many different joint configurations. And I can hold my arm in a particular joint configuration either very stiff or very relaxed. So I have a huge amount of choice to

make. Now it turns out, we are extremely stereotypical and we all move pretty much in the same way. We are so stereotypical that our brains have dedicated neural circuitry to decode this stereotyping.

If I show you some dots on a computer screen and set them in motion with biological based motion, your brain's circuitry would understand instantly what's going on. You will know what this person is doing, whether happy, sad, old, young, which is really a huge amount of information. If the dots just represented cars going around a racing track, you would much have more difficulty identifying what's going on.

The fundamental idea is you want to plan your movements so as to minimise the negative consequence of the noise, and in a way that is recognisable to other people. And as people are going about living their lives, planning movements so as to minimise negative consequences of noise, is a priority objective in accumulating experience.

Your brain has evolved to control movement. And here is the real kicker. **With Neuro-Training techniques we can redirect the sensory and experiential variables to what we want them to be!**

I like to use the example of a touch screen computer as your body and the brain as the operating system. Of course the Nervous System connects the two. Your brain decides what it wants to do and gives a picture on the screen of the options available. It determines what options are available but it doesn't tell you how to use them. You have to get onto the screen and with trial and error you finally work out how to achieve a desired outcome.

The muscles are the touch screen (almost literally) that carry signals to the brain for processing. Unfortunately, the brain will disconnect or deliberately block the signals from the body depending on the context it's operating in.

Yet with a bit of practice, you can use the screen to direct accurate signals to the brain in a way it must pay attention to. Then it not only listens more intently but will act on these specific signals in preference to the old general habitual responses.

The result is a way of getting feedback from the brain via the touch screen (muscles system) that will indicate when an action is having the right effect in the brain.

You can learn how to use the brain to change everything (read 'doing life the hard way') or you can trick the brain into believing the ability is already in the nervous system and ready for it to use.

And as a measure of movement at the body end is registered in the brain as an operating system of that movement the changes come from the brain but it's the body that give those changes the OK.

THE POINT

Two Main Areas of Executive Challenge:

1. **Understanding your influence over change**
2. **Maintaining consistent personal power in all projects**

1. Understanding your influence over change – your Positive influence versus Renegade influence

There is always an influence that you can exert in every situation you direct your attention to, even towards those activities you do not direct attention too but are still responsible for.

We can't get away from the fact that our mind follows our most dominant thought.

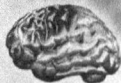

The trouble is, how do we find that dominant thought? As a CEO we often kid ourselves that it's only because we think of something that it must be right for the situation based on our past experience or results we take credit for.

If I told you there was a way to discover any renegade influences before making a decision would you be interested in finding out what that was?

I bet you would, because it can save so much in wasted energy time and eventually money.

As you well know by now, getting clear on your objective is paramount to achieving the long-term results. Working efficiently can become a normal quality instead of an exception that seems to be so elusive for some. Anything that is necessary to achieving a desired end result needs to become a neurological association. Not only an association supporting the process but becoming an active influence in integrating with other resources to compound the effect, in a way that brings congruence back to that process. This creates an internal momentum of neural activity that cannot be measured without the use of a MRI scan.

The subconscious

The best way to access the renegade influences is by using the talents inherent in the subconscious. The subconscious is an amazing device for accumulating information and it already has most if not all the answers you'll ever need. The conscious mind has no chance of keeping up with it and we can train ourselves to use a method to get that information from the subconscious into conscious awareness. Sometimes this happens spontaneously – perhaps you have already experienced times when a decision came 'out of the blue' and ended up being perfect for that situation. The techniques in this book, I am sure, will allow more than enough of those Instinctive decisions to become a normal experience for you.

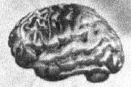

Where do they come from?

You subconscious is a powerful ally and a critical opponent. Learning how to access the subconscious processes is a key to **Instinctive Greatness** and I would suggest the only way to real greatness. To understand greatness, we need a way of understanding the role of the subconscious and only when we have established a clear relationship with our subconscious we can create greatness in any form we choose.

2. Maintaining consistent personal power in all projects

Personal power is a highly misunderstood concept as we are taught to persist until we have made as many mistakes it may take until we finally put together a formula that works. As a consequence, we tend to believe that it's just a matter of hard work and minimising risk that gets us the great results. If you look at the really great results you have achieved, they came mostly from working out what works through experience. If I told you your nervous system has access to options you would take years to find and that you can access those options almost instantly, would you be interested in reducing that learning curve to a third or less?

Yes, the nervous system can be trained to do a task before you have actually experienced or even attempted that task. When you come to do the task later the subconscious has already worked out how to do it in a better way. So why is Neuro-Training different than to say meditation or NLP which claim the same or similar ability?

Neuro-Training takes the changes in the perceptive part of the brain and anchors them into the circuits in the body, so the brain treats the perceptions as a reality. Experience holds greater neurological value than pure perception or imagination. An association between perception and physical action creates a highly valued neurological response that is a higher priority in the brain and will supersede any lesser decisions.

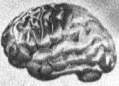

What does this have to do with personal power?

By applying the principles and techniques of **Adaptive Neurology**, your ability is no longer based on the amount of experience you actually have, but rather the amount of **experience you can create** that is relative to achieving what you want. The greater the amount of energy you can put into achieving what you want, the greater the results. Anything that assists you to have more energy and direct that towards your objectives efficiently, the greater will be your personal power.

The limitations are always the conditionings you have associated in your life – you need to find out how they are limiting your energy and power.

There are actually physiological ways to determine them and, as this is a 'hands off' book, we need to generalise this just a bit.

How we overcome the conditioning is to use the same process we use to learn anything in the first place, through Association. We have already been through conditioning that determines our behavioural responses so we can use the same process of association to add new elements or positive conditions to what is already there which then changes the final outcomes.

We take advantage of the mechanisms already in the brain which create new associations, and therefore give the brain more options than it would normally have access to.

One of the critical processes we use in life is with our body's physical experience and how that relates to our feelings and perceptions during that experience. We use the physical sensations of evidence that something is real and exists as a fact in the outside world, and the nervous system adapts to that evidence and then constructs what it needs to achieve your desires.

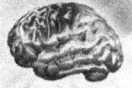

If physical experience does not give us evidence that matches our values then we have a 'negative experience'. When the physical does match our values we have a 'positive experience', and these experiences become the basis of our positive or negative beliefs.

You have probably already heard that all you need to do to change your life is change your beliefs. This would be true if the basic evidence for those beliefs were changed first into what we want them to be, then identify the events that we experienced which laid down foundation of evidence, and then change the conclusion we made about our self or our life by going through that experience. And then rearrange a better perception based on a construction that associates a new more appropriate result for what we want.

Wow what a job, where there is an easy way to get your brain to do it.

The brain already knows all our perceptions, all we have to do is connect them together so as to create new events and relevant meaning.

From a neurological point of view, it is much more important to be clear about what we want than hope it will turn out ok. Clarity of direction is very important for the brain circuits to hook up and conduct the required actions efficiently. The more detail we throw at the mind the more the brain performs for us the way we expect. The more we push our minds the more extended our abilities become and we will start to surprise ourselves with what we are capable of.

All too often we go about things in the opposite way of what would really give us what we want.

I want you to think for a moment about some goal or objectives you want to achieve.

Imagine the goal turning out to be better than you expected.

Notice how that feels to have achieved ten times more than you expected. Good feeling? Ok, give that feeling a colour. A typical response at this point is, "I don't know or I can't see a colour". My typical answer is, "Just imagine a colour that represents that feeling. If you were to imagine there was a colour that represented that feeling what colour would it be?" Using your imagination is a quick version of thinking and is something of a key to the process of achieving your goals ten times faster than you thought. (Of course it is because your thinking is already conditioned to block out options). The nervous system and subconscious respond to imagined experience in the same was as actual experience.

The next step is to see yourself achieving the goal and colour this perception in the same colour you just experienced. Here is where we detour from the normal perceptual processes and add some nifty **Adaptive Neurology** to spice things up a bit. While you are thinking of the perception of you achieving the goal which is still coloured as before look into the Nine Eye Positions and this stimulates your brain to generate more options than you could possibly consciously create. These positions are easily identified if you imagine a square in front of your face. There is an eye position at each corner of the square and at the middle of each side. The ninth position is looking straight forward through the centre of the square.

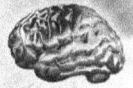

Eye Positions

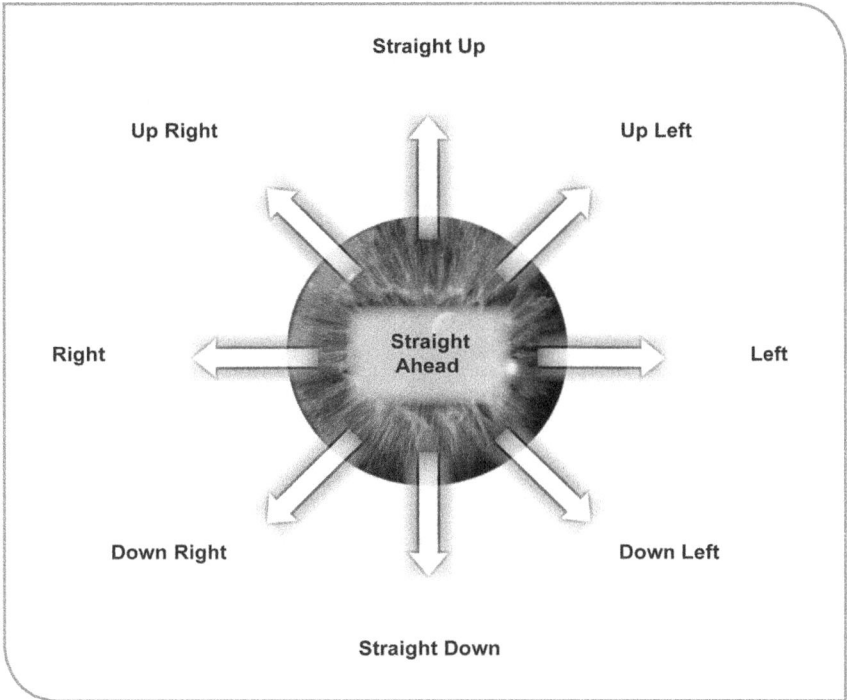

You may find you have to concentrate on the goal and the colour while looking in some of the positions more than others. These positions are where the misperception, limitations and associated stresses exist. This is normal as each eye position is accessing different circuits in your brain and therefore activating different types of information. This information becomes associated with your dominant thought which for this example is you seeing yourself achieving your goals.

The next step is to amplify any positive consequences or feelings from doing this exercise. The feeling of achieving your goals is something that is hardwired into your subconscious and your brain. To activate it

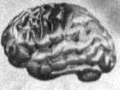

all you need to do is think what that feeling is and we need to anchor that feeling so that it becomes associated to those things that are necessary for achieving your goals internally. This is done by moving the diaphragm with a large breath in and out in each eye position.

If you go to the techniques section in the back of this book you will see this described in more detail in the options generator section.

Chapter 6

YOU ARE NOT YOUR BEHAVIOURS

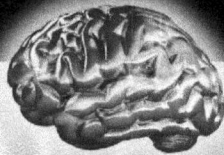

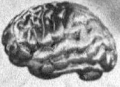

Chapter 6

YOU ARE NOT YOUR BEHAVIOURS

> "To exist is to change, to change is to mature,
> to mature is to go on creating oneself endlessly."
>
> Henri Bergson

I don't know who you are, where you live or what you do, and I don't need to because there have always been situations that have the potential to create stress in your life. My job is to help you find the best challenges for you to overcome and train your nervous system in the best possible way.

No matter what happens in life you are always changing whether you know it or not. You are built in such a way that you cannot not change. You simply develop perceptions that you believe you are not changing by repeating the familiar. To repeat anything, you are still changing something.

Almost any situation can stimulate you to create stress reactions as a way of handling, or not handling, the situation. Your conditioning will trigger a reaction and make anything stressful. You see, it's not what the situation is but rather your reaction to it, which in most part is activated by your own existing conditioning. How you deal with the situation determines the effect it is going to have on you. Are you reinforcing a positive conditioning or a negative conditioning? Either way you are training yourself to do 'something' better. How you deal with stressful reactions is on a subconscious level which uses no conscious awareness.

While you remain a victim to your conditioning, (read 'neurology of your body'), you continue to be unaware of your influence on your life and its success. If you are not aware, then your body simply does what it has been conditioned to do. That is to react to external stimuli. Often you will fail to notice the affect this is having on your body until the stress levels reach a certain, critical, point when your body tells you in no uncertain terms, that it is not comfortable.

The resultant discomfort acts as a warning that, if you continue ignoring the problem, things will get worse! You may then look for solutions to take away the discomfort or pain and settle for anything that alleviates the issue. The trouble is you are trying to fix something from within a stressed and dysfunctional state. You may feel better temporarily, but the root cause remains.

When the brain identifies a stressful situation, a cascade of chemical reactions take place that encourages your body to produce even more chemicals. You may be too busy to notice these changes but you will notice a change in eating or addictive behaviours.

Changing your thoughts is an obvious answer to reducing the amount of stressful chemicals in the body, yet, if you are not even aware of the thought process that has allowed stress to accumulate in your body then you are hardly in a position to 'change your mind'. Trying to make these types of changes mentally is like asking a blind man for directions. He will tell you – but not in the way you expect!

Your body, nervous system and brain will heal themselves given the right environment to do so, and the chemicals associated with stress would not have to accumulate in your body. The result is – different actions will follow.

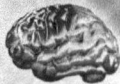

We all have subconscious conditioning that impacts upon us, beginning during childhood. It maybe genetic or acquired. The messages you learn in your early years are references you use to navigate your way through life and the world. You cannot turn the clock back, but you can begin to take conscious control again and change the way your past affects your current processing. Eventually or sometimes instantaneously, you will change how you relate to the various stimuli encountered on a daily basis.

When you are triggered by a subconscious memory that, at the same time, you judge as stressful, you are simply following learnt behaviour and reacting to a memory, not an actual threat. It is this reactive conditioning that you experience as stress as it builds in our nervous and glandular systems. This creates the habit of identification with the feelings that perpetuate the uncomfortable feeling.

While you still think the problems you encounter are all external to yourself you will continue to try to 'fix' the problem, either by running away, denial, or doing something, if just to alleviate and numb the sensory input.

The real cause of stress is the subconscious deciding to prove what happened to you when you were young is more relevant than what's happening now! It uses your body's conditioning as justification to maintain the reaction to external stimuli.

You will see many methods later in this book – some will be more successful at various times than others – which are all a way of training the subconscious to use different solutions and pathways to resolve an issue.

The less you judge yourself or others the less polarised your consciousness. The less polarised you are the less you experience situations that may have previously caused you to go into a stress reaction.

The less you experience stressful situations the more your body relaxes, the more your body relaxes the faster it recuperates.

With continued practice of these techniques, problems that existed before simply cease to exist. There is then no need to find a way to 'deal' with stress because stress is no longer a part of your reaction to life.

Coping with Coping Skills

With the ever increasing number of types of stress, comes an ever-increasing number of coping skills. Oh my goodness, what a dilemma we have now. Too many stresses combined with too many coping skills.

When I look through the multitude of coping skills I am amazed that people cannot see that most of them are just common sense! When you are 'stressed' you cannot think straight so these coping strategies could seem like a good answer. But generally the wrong question is being asked.

Instead of asking, "How can I cope with this stress?", in other words, how can I learn how to meet expectations and how to operate well enough to live with the stress, you should be asking, "What is a stress reaction and what can I do to stop it from happening before I need to learn to cope with its effects?"

The problem with the general approach to coping is that it distracts you away from seeing stress reactions for what they are and by engaging in many of these coping 'skills' you can easily suppress the expression of the stress reaction and fail to reach its cause.

Understand better by understanding the facts

We all have a genetic system that gives us two arms, two legs, one liver and one head, etc. That represents the basic genetic package you get when conceived. Also, with that package comes a mountain of learned adaptive behaviours from your parents and their forebears.

Most of that extra behavioural information will never become active in our lives, except under unique circumstances, when they take on a life of their own. Most of your early life experiences are reinforcing the inherited behaviours, firstly of mum and dad, secondly from further up in the family tree. There is a sea of possibilities just sitting inside you waiting to be activated.

Continued stress reactions will eventually lead to activating the information stored in your genetic system. The combination of the stress reactions and the use of the wrong coping skills will suppress your ability to resolve the challenges and activate inherited weaknesses. Appearing as sudden or even slow onset diseases, these symptoms are a result of the suppression of stress reactions that relate to something you have inherited that is not a good answer.

Everyone generally agrees that stress is a health hazard. But very few people make the link between suppressed stresses leading to disease patterns being activated. This becomes even more relevant when you see people using strong medication to suppress the reactions because they are afraid of the pain or they are irritated by annoying symptoms aggravating their lives.

Any coping skill can suppress a distress if you are sensitive to that type of coping skill. Because of what is already in your nervous and genetic systems, you will have certain preferences in life and certain desires to express. These sensitivities are usually unknown until you try one of

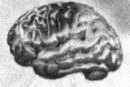

these coping skills. By then it may be too late to reverse the suppression that can take place under these circumstances.

There is a way to 'buffer' the effects of having an inherited mine field built into your genetic system. Remind the subconscious to only access the positive supportive habits also built into the genetic system. Common sense strategies, and I refer here to positive coping skills, should be used according to the challenges being tackled rather than as a general solution to a stress reaction. "Positive" or "Negative" coping skills are a judgment call. In the subconscious there is no such thing as positive or negative, only relevant or irrelevant.

Suppression is one of the most, if not *the* most, dangerous activities humans can engage in.

We are all designed to express our nature. Our nervous system's job is to express ourselves and experience other people's expression through our senses. That includes mental expression, emotional expression and physical expression. Anything that reduces or eliminates our ability to express, suppresses our most basic needs.

If ten people have a headache, they will be told to have an aspro or paracetamol or some other type of painkiller. Yet how would it be possible that all ten people would have the same cause for their headache and require that specific medication to resolve it? In fact, there would be ten different reasons for the ten headaches and therefore at least a different range of solutions for these people to resolve the headache. More likely there would be ten different solutions. Yes, the pain may go away, but is that not "shooting the messenger"? If you use pain (physical, mental or emotional) as the guiding criteria for eliminating stress, you can easily prescribe or be prescribed a solution that will suppress the real issue and therefore create a continuance of the problem, not a solution.

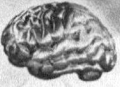

We tend not to recognise the suppressive activities that have happened to us and what effect it has had either. Even if you do recognise it, you ignore it because of how you have been trained in society and family life. This has an accumulative effect that makes it even easier for distress to occur and get stronger with time. So now you would have two problems to deal with, the accumulation of stress reactions and the accumulation of suppressions of various types. This is a deadly combination because the stress reactions (distress) will stop us from recuperating effectively, limiting our ability to overcome any challenge and the suppression challenging our vital functions and distorting them into something that is far more demanding.

On top of that, the suppression is the fastest way to activate any inherited patterns that could eventually be the cause of your death. I don't know about you, but when I die I want it to be as easy as possible. You don't have to be sick to die. You are in dangerous waters when you activate the inherited references in the genetic system. All of these references are from your ancestors and there is absolutely no doubt that they all did one thing, die! So if you are activating any of these references it is very easy to accidentally 'trip over' an inherited pattern of activity that will be the cause of your death.

Stress is the groundwork for disease

The reason I write this book is not to show you ways of feeling better when you are stressed, but rather to point out that distress (your reaction to stress) causes depletion in your ability to recuperate from what your nervous system has learned from your past experiences.

And that while suppression continues to affect your functions, your energy is used to compensate rather than resolve, which will eat up your energy faster than you can make it. Eventually you will not have enough energy production and activation of genetic patterns will become a fact, not a possibility.

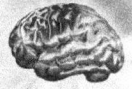

This is an overview of how people are dying slowly, and progressing further and further into an irreversible conclusion. This has lead people to believe that when they get old, they become sick, they die.

If you keep the recuperation high and turn it into a habit, you can stay on top of life's challenges and never get to the stage of activating any genetic patterns and therefore eliminate the onset of disease.

If you look closely at the 'diseases' today, you will see they are mostly 'dysfunctions' not diseases. Any dysfunction can be reorganised to become functional again. Once a dysfunction has progressed past the point of no return, and this is done by suppressing the dysfunction instead of re-instigating proper function, it makes structural changes in the person and their recovery is much more difficult. It is guaranteed that disease will follow.

Any life-threatening process is a progression of events that lead to its development. All of these progressions start with distress at their base. As the distress continues, the recuperation dwindles till eventually there is little the immune system can do to reverse the effect.

Self-medication – to self-abuse and suppression of symptoms

Self-medication and the accumulation of previously prescribed medicines is problem enough. Its main effect is to reduce or change the symptoms to something the person may accept or they expect that the symptoms will change eventually and so keep taking the medications.

Medication vary rarely resolves many issues especially if the causative origins are emotional or mental rather than chemical. Medications are deliberately suppressive and usually irrelevant to solving the cause but just a way of covering up the 'signals' the subconscious is sending.

If chemicals didn't cause the problem, how are they going to fix it?

The only true management procedures are those which continue to monitor the levels of stress as a way of taking the opportunity to find the best way to eliminate it. Any other management is wasting time and resources that defy the supposition that stress is an unwanted factor in our lives.

The secret that could save your life

Here is the secret that can prolong your life and cure the problems of the world.

Oh, yes, sure, this is going to cure the world's problems, sure?

It's True!

If you can accept that suppression means the repression of expression of our real selves and the consequent effects of that as a negative thing, you can act on that knowledge to bring about positive changes in how you operate in life, then, your life will be better and longer.

There is a direct and inverse correlation between suppression and the quality of our life experiences.

My own experience of life includes the misplaced responsibility I was given as the firstborn child and the consequent compensations I developed to adjust to that situation. Later in life I looked back at that situation with 20/20 hindsight and realised how 'my true nature' had been suppressed and how that led me to have patterns of behaviour I did not want to have.

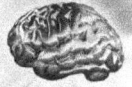

Luckily by that time I had learned skills that could help me change the neurological response to the stress of being the 'firstborn' and its 'built-in' responsibilities. I thought it must be really difficult for anyone without these skills to overcome the inherent stress reactions that are activated every day because of 'old' situations.

Your subconscious does not forget anything and is always rewriting the past to fit into current value structures. So even if you think you have 'gotten over it', your nervous system and subconscious have not.

The reason I say suppression is the 'last stage' is because if you do not change the suppression it will build up a huge amount of compensation all of which are using your vital energy until you have too little to help you deal with daily tasks.

On the contrary, if you are able to change the effect of the suppression by eliminating it completely, you will have released the use of the energy and have a massive injection of new power.

It occurred to me that if I had the choice between dying of some old experience or living longer with more energy, I choose the latter.

I studied and researched until I found a foolproof way of removing those suppressions. Neuro-Training is the result of that research. It has grown out of the need to find a solution to the thousands of suppressions you accumulate through your life that will eventually kill you.

Do you have too many options?

Suppression is the reason why there are so many different health modalities around today. The discussion about the relationship between them must wait for another book, but, nonetheless, the argument still stands true that there is no one panacea for everyone's needs.

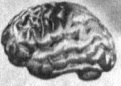

Yet at the same time we are all using the same systems to create and maintain our symptoms.

Discovering that the 'Internal Systems' all work the same way, but to varying degrees, was a milestone in the journey to developing Neuro-Training. It's not a panacea approach because the Nervous System is an open system in itself, which moulds around your experience and helps you make new realisations and connections within and between existing internal (innate) systems.

Your body is designed to work with your subconscious to create a symphony of coordination and integration. The systems do this by using the resources within the subconscious and memory as a library from which to draw. Within this library are also the distress experiences that will make the 'symphony' play the wrong sounds at the wrong times.

You need to know about the symphony and what music it is able to create because this has the essence of your conflicts buried within it. There is a very easy way to listen to your symphony and your body holds the key.

Chapter 7

PERFECT PRACTICE MAKES PERFECT SENSES

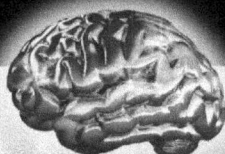

Chapter 7

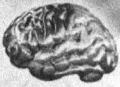

PERFECT PRACTICE MAKES PERFECT SENSES

> "Everyone who means well gives advice based on his or her perception. I have realized that while it's important to hear the suggestions, one should only listen to oneself."
>
> Emraan Hashmi

Train Your Inner Nervous System To Work... For You!!

Wake up time for your nervous system!

Everything I have written about in this book has so far been interesting wordage. Without a practical way of taking your nervous system by the horns, you can't take true advantage over the challenges in your life from the past and into the future.

In your nervous system there is no such thing as past and future, only relative or not relative.

You can and should take everything I have said that triggers any kind of resonance inside you and apply the techniques to those triggers. Who cares what your life has been? That's never going to change, so why worry about or be influenced by the past? Because you have become conditioned by your response to that past and those responses are built into your nervous system.

Instinctive greatness comes from creating a mode of operating that is designed to achieve what you set out to achieve AND which changes the conditioning within at the same time.

To change the past conditioning, you do these techniques while focusing on the effects and experiences of the past. To design your future, you focus on what it is you want in many different time frames and see the ongoing influence of your design building its momentum.

There are many references in your mind that you would not tolerate paying any conscious attention to now, but as time goes on and you realise that your reality is created and maintained by you and you can change that reality from the inside out, you will create as a natural expression of being who you are.

Nelson Mandela had it right when he said we are afraid of our own power. So we find ways to trap it, limit it, distort it, forget about it and fill our lives with irrelevant garbage.

Make a pact with yourself to do at least a different one of these techniques every day and take note of how your thoughts change, feelings become more secure, your actions feel natural and obvious and at last you feel free to be.

It's then you know your influence on yourself is mastered. Then you can help others master their influence on themselves.

Follow the instructions and you'll set yourself free. Enjoy.

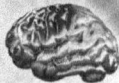

TABLE OF EXERCISES

The Master List for your exercises:

Use any one of these as your focus with any exercise here. Focus on the sentence even by saying it over and over while you do the exercises. Use one sentence with each exercise to get the greatest results. Of course if want to use any other statement you are more than welcome to use that.

- How to double the energy you devote to running the show when you need it. Have energy on tap.

- How to create certainty of mind in all your business decisions.

- Your personal psychology of doing what's right.

- How to create breakthrough systems and structures 'out of the blue'.

- How to break through company politics with relevant and unique communication.

- Five key health practices mean you will never worry about your health again.

- How to smash through the, "Nobody can do it better than me", syndrome.

- How to tap into learning and processes of change for success.

- Your essential position with money to attract investors and clients to accelerate your growth.

- Insider secrets to keeping your brain working at 100% to produce clear, sharp, clever decisions.

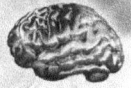

- Shortcuts to being great even though you do it easier than anyone else.

- How your focus can make it easier to make more than staying at the level you are now.

- How to empower your future by applying Adaptive Neurology.

- How to guide others to a better future with your influence.

Or use any of these statements with the exercises

Planning ahead Goal strategy

Think empowering thoughts	Attitude for achieving goals
Eliminate toxins	Clean your body of past experience
Exercise	Prepare for greater ability
Eating well	Prepare for greater support
Rest, Relax and Rejuvenate	Recuperate from your labour
Evaluate	Reassess to start again
Sleep	Disciplining your mind etc.

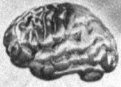

INTRODUCTION

In the first part of this book you were exposed to 'Stress Elimination', you learned a great deal about stress and hopefully a great deal about yourself.

You now have some choices to make. You can take the information you learned and store it in your subconscious amongst all those stress files, or you can continue on and use the knowledge you have gained and put it into practice.

You may be asking yourself "how am I going to do that?" Your brain probably feels like it is going to explode if you were to implement the new concepts so far. Well here is the perfect way to take the pressure off. Getting into action is going to make life a whole lot simpler, and a whole lot more enjoyable and successful.

So go for it – it's your life and you are in control… or at least you will be at the end of these exercises.

SECTION 1 – PRACTICAL APPLICATIONS
AND TECHNIQUES

You will find this book offers you tons of choices. So let's get started.

Exercise 1: Changing the Quality of Life

So how much do you think you can increase the quality of your life and business? Well that is entirely your choice and up to you. If you do this exercise occasionally then you are going to get some changes. On the other hand, if you aggressively follow this exercise you are going to get some major life changes. It's really up to you!!

Just so you know, not only are you going to be getting rid of stress (not just control it) you are going to recognise potential in yourself you never knew was there. Life is dependent on how well you can identify, experience and express your values.

What's the Value?

In this exercise you are going to ask yourself a series of questions, and then you must give some real thought to the answers. The internal processes you use to answer these questions is based on your innermost values. Your nervous system has the sole job of processing your values into a communicable form. You don't have to consciously know what your values are but it helps if you have some idea of what your nervous system is trying to do.

While answering these questions ad as much sensory description as you can to your answers. See yourself doing, being or having the answer. Hear the voices of those around you applauding your success. Listen to the other sounds that would remind you of the effect of this answer

in your life. Feel the sensations of achieving the answers in a way that you would want to have and amplify those feelings. How would you be breathing if you felt that way one hundred times more?

Imagine the smells that would associate to the answers becoming true for you. What aromas are around, what perfumes of significant others do you notice?

Notice what actions you would be taking in fulfilling those answers to their ultimate. Notice how the answers have changed your life into the best life you could possibly have.

Do whatever you have to do to make the results of your answers real and true for you. Notice how others agree with your truth and reality and support your reality and adopt your reality as their own.

Answer these questions with the sensory input as above, and we will use them as a way to challenge your nervous system's ability to express who it thinks you are more efficiently.

Question #1 – *"If I had no stress reactions what would my life be like?"*

Now in order to answer this question, apply it to the different areas of your life and concentrate on the physical, emotional, and mental stress related to those areas. So what would it be like if there were no stress reactions?

- In your marriage.

- With your kids.

- At work, etc.

Now continue writing the answer to this question for each area of life and do the same for each question.

Question #2 – *"What would I be doing differently if I had no stress?"*

Question #3 – *"If I could imagine there were other things I would be doing with my life what would they be?"*

Again, apply this question and answer it for each of the categories you listed above.

Make sure you give these questions lots of thought. For Question #3, make a detailed list, no matter how insignificant you may consider the thought to be. Be sure to make a list as we will need this later on in the book.

Two things are going to take place in going through these processes. Your concept of the past is going to change, and your future is going to become the way you want it.

The focus of this exercise is to reset your values. When you are in stress reactions you cannot possibly think clearly enough to achieve this. That's why you can never naturally get a total solution to stress challenges. The goal is to follow the values that you are going to set for yourself then let them lead you to your end goal.

You are now going to learn is how to understand why things happen the way they do and the reason why some things just don't happen. This is part of a Neuro-Training exercise based on restructuring your reality.

Value Structure

This is your first stepping stone to reset the values that drive your nervous system to behave the way it does. It provides the foundation for changing the way you react to your challenges by re-routing your thoughts to what's important in your life.

Resetting the Value Structure changes the basis of your behaviour.

Just what is a value?

A value is something we use energy to get or go towards either a thing, person or experience. It can also be the opposite. It can be something we expend energy to get away from, someone, something or experience. Values stimulate the structures in the limbic part of your brain which puts this exercise into the Pleasure–Pain context. Going towards pleasure and away from pain.

To make it simple:

Positive values equal things you want to aim for

Negative values equal what you want to avoid

Ok, back to work.

While you are working through these next few steps just focus on what you are writing without thinking too much about the process, just focus on the content.

Make a list of all your good values and try to list at least nine if not more. These could also be values you see in others and would like to have as your own. Try to think of at least nine values.

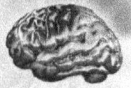

Look at the first one you wrote and ask yourself if it's more important than the second item on your list. If "Yes", compare the first entry with the third and as long as you keep answering 'yes' keep going down the list.

If you answer with a "No", this means that entry has more value than the first one.

Now the focus is on the value you just found (the "No" response value) and how it relates to the rest on your list.

Keep going through your list this way. As soon as you have found a value that is more important than all the others, place it on a new list and remove it from the old list. Then go back to the original list and starting at the top repeat the process again.

Continue this exercise until you have all the values from the old list moved to the second list that is showing the values in descending order of importance.

Here is what happens ...

The values you have at the top of your second list are the ones that are the most important to your subconscious. No matter what takes place these values have priority. Your nervous system will strive to accomplish these values.

Once you clearly understand these values you will find a lot less stress, confusion and inner conflicts going on.

You can do this for different areas of life and see if there are some values trying to be expressed in the wrong context. This is the first lesson to thinking clearer and knowing yourself better.

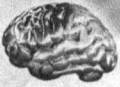

As an example, a man was having trouble finding a lifetime partner. His business was to buy and sell businesses and it took most of his time (65 hours a week).

When we did a Value Structure with him we found values like:

Sharing, Communication, Working together, Successful, Profitable, Growing, Money, Opportunity and Fulfilling.

This is an interesting list of values but as a basis for a relationship not as good as they could be and just as easily be a list of values for a business venture. I asked him where is 'love, companionship, intimacy', and all the other things that may be more important for a relationship to work. The only thing close to a relationship value here is sharing and communication. I didn't ask if that meant holding shares in the relationship, I think I knew the answer.

We then had to reinvent relationships for this man by getting him to act on one of the highest values in his list. He chose communication.

After much discussion and reinventing himself he finally asked her out. And yes they lived happily ever after.

You can see from this how the values of his business world had 'taken over' his other value structures. It was important for him to start to develop a new set of values at the same time recognising what value structures were already in place.

You don't want to change the values structures too radically, just work with what is there first then move onto other values as you can. This exercise will give you a clearer picture of what your subconscious thinks 'should be'. You can then decide you want to change it or not, that's your call.

Just by going through this exercise, you are practicing making a 'Decision'. It is very important that this decision-making is practiced by you for you, by choice first. When you are clear about your values and can make decisions as to which ones you want or don't want, you regain control over your 'subconscious' life again.

If you have any questions on how to do this or what to do with it, leave me a message on the website, www.TheEfficientCEOBrain.com and I'll help you with the process.

At this point you should have a list of answers to the questions posed earlier and a list of the most important values about yourself. We will utilise these later as we go further into the workings of your subconscious.

SECTION 2 – TRAINING YOUR SUBCONSCIOUS IN WAYS IT CAN'T REFUSE

Neuro-Training is developing Adaptive Neurology and creates what I call Neurological Intelligence.

The next few chapters will be devoted to explaining the practical side of Eliminating Stress Reactions with proven techniques and processes that will free you from Stress, Depression and Anxiety in a way that your subconscious and nervous system recognises as real.

I call these 'Better Neurological Options' because not all of these will have the same effect with every person. So what works for one person may not work the same way for another. I have added a number of these 'options' so you can play with them until you find a 'nice' combination that suits you.

It's not hard and doing any of them can only make you better. What makes them 'better' is their relevance to your nature rather than the effect they have in and of themselves. They are all neurological in essence because they have been discovered by working with real live people. And what makes them so powerful is that they will always have some beneficial effect.

I will give you the best one first, which is called the **'Options Generator'**.

The reason this is the best one, in my opinion, is because it has the ability to change the subconscious perceptions of whatever stress you are focusing on. Your subconscious is able to create an enormous amount of ideas and its own 'options' much faster and more efficiently than you can consciously. But even though it can do that, you naturally limit the number of these options you actually create.

Beliefs, fears and habits keep us from allowing these new options to be given a 'fair go' in the subconscious. This option is able to shortcut the limitation process and allows the subconscious to have access to the new options long enough for it to decide which ones are the best options to take and put into action within its own circuits.

You are lucky that the subconscious will always do the best it can for you with what it has at its disposal. This option gives it more to play with and therefore gives you more and better options.

It is like giving your subconscious the permission to come up with a ton of possibilities and then selecting the best one. It's all done automatically. And it will be the best because you cannot know consciously all the factors involved with any specific situation, yet the subconscious knows everything about it.

This option gives us a chance to stand back and really see what the subconscious is capable of. I am proud to say that it includes a process that I developed two decades ago which has been adopted by other health care modalities – Eye Modes and Breathing.

This is for people who want to live a full life, but can't get started...

Exercise 2: Getting started with the 'Options Generator'

The brain will create some amazing options in your life and it does so automatically. You can use its ability to generate new options by stimulating those parts of the brain responsible for your creative processes. Under the right circumstances your brain will create more options than you could ever consciously think of in a lifetime. It's an easy process and can be done by anyone who wants to change something that's not 'right' in their life.

The 'Options Generator' can be used with any other 'techniques' you already know, and that's why this is such an important amplifier of

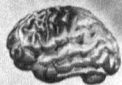

change. This can be adapted to, and used in conjunction with, any other Innate System, health care technique, NLP process, yoga procedure or anything else that helps your change your behaviours. It works partly by helping to create new options which means new perceptions related to any issue or goal you might have, and associates these with the techniques you are using. With this technique you have the ability to retrain your subconscious responses relative to anything you focus on during the process.

The sooner you learn how to do this as a daily activity, the faster you will experience the changes.

Let's get straight into the technique.

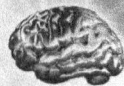

You can have someone help you as above or do the holding yourself. It makes no difference who holds the head but it is mandatory to do these exercises holding the front and back of your head, don't forget. If you don't do the holding the brain will go off into its old reactions and you will reinforce the stress reaction.

This image or map for the eye positions you can use to place your eyes in the right directions is on page 101.

I left the lines a little long to remind you to look as far as possible into these directions.

If you were to imagine a vertical line and a horizontal line running through the centre of the square. Where these two lines cross the square at the edges, the corners and its centre are the main eye positions to place your eyes. Just follow the numbers.

Access new options with Eye Positions

While you are looking in these positions, focus your thoughts on something you want to change in our life. Your brain will then create a new set of responses related to what you are focusing on.

Your brain can process solutions faster than you can consciously think, so just let it take over and create whatever solutions it wants. You probably won't become consciously aware of any solutions to start with. Then again, you may. That's not all there is to it and I would think you would really want to get the most out of this, right?

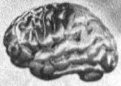

Extend your options

To extend the ability of the subconscious to expand the number and type of solutions it can create, lets add a couple of extra components to this process.

Firstly, and probably the most important part of this, is to hold the front and back of your head. No, this is not voodoo, witchcraft or 'hocus pocus', but it does have a remarkable ability to keep the energy, blood and nutrients in the brain while it is doing its amazing job.

It's simple really. As you look in the different eye positions (following the numbers) you continue to hold the front and back of your head. For ease of doing the process, move your eyes through the positions in a clockwise direction and then in an anti-clockwise direction (go backwards through the numbers). All the time keep holding the front and back of your head.

The reason for this is a simple neurological phenomenon. When the eyes are placed in certain positions they access different brain activities or functions. At the same time holding the head is stimulating the brain to create new ideas and options in the frontal lobes. The combination of the two means the options being created are then connected with all the different functions that the eyes are accessing. That's a lot of options and new connections! Then the subconscious can choose the best option for the challenge you are thinking about.

But why would the subconscious choose any of them? It's familiar with what it has been doing and would prefer to continue along the same old habitual pathway right?

Exactly!

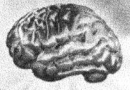

That's why you have to up the 'value stakes' related to these new options. Remember you cannot possibly consciously know all of the options the brain can create but you can make the subconscious believe they are important. So to do that you associate what's happening in the brain with something you know is important to it, like say, breathing.

As you are looking in each eye position, take a deep breath in and out. Not just a little breath, make it a big huge one where you have to really use your lungs and diaphragm. Now you will have all those nice new ideas anchored to the important function of breathing as well as to the action of one of the most important and largest muscles in your body, the diaphragm. Your subconscious is going to sit up and pay attention to those new options now with renewed vigour. Now it will select the better option because your subconscious is an opportunist.

I mentioned before about looking in the various positions going clockwise then anticlockwise. There seems to be some other functions the brain accesses when moving in a general direction, but also when the eyes are closed or open. So you add to this strange mix the element of doing the whole process with the eyes closed as well as you just saw, with the eyes open. It seems this has to do with some glandular activity of the brain and stimulates more biochemical associations to the new options.

Instead of waiting till it's too late, I will give you some specific activities to do while using the different eye positions so you can get more benefit from the process. Your life can be reorganised using this mental software if you just apply yourself. Never take life seriously. Nobody gets out of it alive anyway.

When you feel stressed, use the Options Generator thinking only of the stressful feeling, thing, person or circumstance that stresses you. Remember to only do this while holding the front and back of your head, do NOT do this without holding your head!

Then repeat the Options Generator while thinking of how you would like the situation to turn out. With as much detail as possible. At this stage it's OK to exaggerate the positive outcome as much as you want. Again, this is to stimulate your brain and subconscious to create new and better options so why hold it back?

This will give your subconscious a greater scope of references when it's creating new alternatives to the existing patterns as well as give you the freedom of thought to apply the new options it creates. In whatever circumstances you had stress before, this process will change your internal cognitive responses and help your subconscious create better and more appropriate options.

Use this with every stressor you can think of. Eventually it will be very difficult for you to get stressed. In the 60s, people took 'acid' to make the world weird. Now the world is weird and people take Prozac to make it normal!

Exercise Three: Options Generator + Your relationship with natural and artificial chemicals.

This brings me to the effect that chemical substances can have on your perception and therefore your responses to every day challenges. I think most people are aware that the quality of what they put in their body is going to have a direct influence on the quality of the experiences they have through life.

You have probably heard the statement, "You are what you eat", but I would suggest that it should read, "You are what you retain". The more junk and processed foods you retain the more you will 'bend' the natural direction of your biochemical functions to have to compensate.

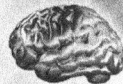

These become patterns of behaviour and of course even the best of foods these days have about half the vitamins and minerals than they did in 1975. Plus, now there are so many additives in the foods they are not really food anymore, rather chemical mixtures. So even looking to food as a way of helping your stress levels is actually going to maintain or even aggravate your reactions.

It's not hard, it's just necessary!

What to do?

Take the foods you eat everyday first and hold them next to your skin somewhere, a cheek is good. Now do your Options Generator while thinking of the food's nutrition being absorbed completely and the unwanted remains being eliminated completely.

It's amazing what thoughts come to your mind during the process. Any inappropriate associations to the foods will 'come to the surface' and be recognised by the subconscious as unnecessary. People have reported the elimination of allergy reactions using this process and it works consistently well for any old memories that are still influencing your behaviours and feelings.

A friend once relayed this story of when she had broken up with her boyfriend of 4 years... and was devastated. She came home after work (left early) and came home for some consolation from mum. As she had always used food as a self-medication to overcome the symptoms of emotional stress, she reached for whatever food was available. The only food in the house at the time was Champagne and Chocolate Éclairs (a type of very rich pastry). So she and her mother ate and drank these until they were both violently ill.

To this day neither of them have eaten Éclairs or drank Champagne since!

These associations to the negative emotional circumstances and the processes of digesting some rather strange foods leave a lifelong impression.

Doing the Options Generator will change the stress reactions to those foods and especially the emotional reactions that were associated at the time. Just because you use the Options Generator with some food/s, does NOT mean you have to engage in consuming the foods.

This is not an 'either–or' situation!

It simply means that whatever reactions were locked into the nervous system at the time can be changed. The effect of that can be too numerous to mention. Don't eat anything you have used this technique with for at least 14 days. That gives the biochemistry time to 'catch up'.

Exercise Four: Options Generator + Your Past

Think of the stages of your life from now till five minutes before your demise. Look back towards now and see what you did in your life. With whom, what you would keep and what you would change.

See yourself taking the steps to make those changes now. What effect do they have on your life and the things you want to achieve before you go?

Now use the Options Generator to plug those wanted parts of your life right back into the subconscious and watch what you do with them.

By all means use your imagination!

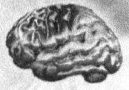

Imagine how you would like your life to be in 5, 10, and 15 or 20 years from now with as much details as you can create. Go through the Options Generator with this perception in mind and let your subconscious run free in its ability to create something for you. Then see what your subconscious does with that!

OK let's make a summary for you.

1. Decide what you want to focus on, from the exercises above. You don't have to just focus on what stresses you, it can be something you want in your life or something you want to improve the quality of. In making these decisions, always think of as many other options and possibilities would be of benefit to work with. MAKE A LIST! So you will never miss out on any of those good things that come to your mind.

2. Hold the front and back of your head and move your eyes into the first position. (It does not matter which eye position you start in). If what you think of is a stress, make it even worse in your mind until it starts to change or even disappear. If you are thinking of something you want to improve on, make it worse first just like you did with the stress, and then make it better than you ever thought it could be. While still in that eye position, take a big breath in and out.

3. Go to the next eye position and do the same process as before until you either feel good about the theme or it just doesn't seem to be important any more. Take your big breath in and out.

4. Continue to the next eye position and repeat the process again. Always think of the original stress or theme in each eye position first. Holding the front and back of your head the whole time.

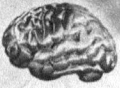

5. Once you have been through all the eye positions (including straight forward), go through the positions again in the opposite direction.

6. Now that you have been through all eye positions in both directions with your eyes open, now do them all again with your eyes closed.

Yes, I know it sounds a bit laborious but after a little practice you will be able to fly through stress issues faster than lightning. Start noticing when you get stressed during the day and make a list of 'homework' to do every day. It won't take long before you will have 'caught up' with all the old stress patterns and booted them into oblivion.

Guess what? You can do the Options Generator with any future projects or goals. Don't hold back with the imagination either. The more you can 'put into it' the more you will get from it.

This is an exercise for your imagination that will produce some very amazing responses in and for you.

Please let me know what changes in your experience I really am interested in your ability to change. So do me a favour and drop me a line at andrew@theefficientceobrain.com with some good news.

Enjoy!

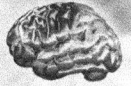

SECTION 3 – THE DICHOTOMY OPTION

This special bonus to add to your neurological tool-kit has a chapter all to itself.

One of the unique qualities humans have when they are stressed is that their two brain hemispheres do not function together as one whole unit. When the two sides function independently or worse, one side dominates over the other; you will exhibit more dichotomies in your behaviour.

Definition of Dichotomy

Being twofold: a classification into two opposed parts or subclasses possibly acting at the same time.

In simple terms and how this relates in a more practical way, you would define dichotomy as two opposites existing at the same time. In effect, a person is attempting to do one thing while the opposite is occurring. Dichotomy is the reason why goals don't work. Dichotomies are the reason why you can work so hard to do something and continually find the opposite result to what you want.

People will often **say** they will do one thing and then actually **do** the opposite. But the amazing part of dichotomy is that when people are doing these behaviours they don't recognise they are doing them. It's like a hypnotic state that takes over and while you think you are doing the 'right' thing, the larger picture is falling apart.

Sometimes this can be explained by being focused on the details and missing the larger context. Yes, that does happen too but that is not dichotomy. Traditional Chinese Medicine call this the coexistence of yin and yang. That the opposites live inside everything and it's our job to find which side you need to be on, getting stuck in neither side.

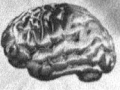

Herein lays the essence of the technique I will show you now. It does not stop you from being yin or yang, positive or negative, hot or cold, etc. It does allow you to move from one side of the dichotomy to the other. In doing so you can move again with freedom from one experience to another without your subconscious trying to get you to see some specific point it wants to make.

This has been referred to as a psychological reversal or psychological conflict. These are two states of attitude that resist your attempts to do or be what you want.

I often hear overweight people say they want to be thin but at the same time they are eating a cream, jam-filled donut. This is an example of a psychological conflict. An example of a psychological reversal is when the overweight person says they want to be fat even though they know it's bad for them.

In either case there is a big problem to overcome. Not the overweight or the fear or the mother-in-law (oops, sorry mum). The problem to first resolve is this dichotomy of behaviour that leads to opposite behaviours being lived out.

The Chinese found that for many psychological disturbances, the best way to progress is to treat the heart and kidneys. In Traditional Chinese Medicine these two control the head and if these two are in balance, the head energy will be in balance also.

That's nice but playing around with the heart energy can cause other problems. So instead of manipulating the heart directly they found that working with the energetic brother organ to the heart, the Small Intestine, they were able to balance the energy to the head without disturbing the heart. Pretty smart people I think.

The result is that over thousands of years the Chinese have been using a variety of techniques to balance the head (thinking) by manipulating the Small Intestine energy flow. Today this has been condensed down in to a few good consistent techniques that work for everyone.

The most effective of these techniques I will show you now.

Before I do, though, there are a few words I need to share with you so you understand some important distinctions between this and some other 'techniques' out there. This technique is specific for dichotomy. It is not a technique I recommend for any problem. In fact, I would suggest you don't just do this because it seems like a good idea for anything other than a dichotomy related attitude or behaviour. (When two opposites seem to be occurring)

It is still up to you to decide what a dichotomy is and what isn't. And if you are not sure, I would say do this rather than not do it. But don't fall into the trap of using this for any and everything that seems to be a problem.

Unfortunately, it has become a bit of a 'fad' to use this technique as a 'fix-all' rather than as one option in a possibly complicated story. The technique requires you to tap certain acupuncture points that relate to the Small Intestine energy flow in your body. There are people teaching how to use 'tapping points' to solve everything under the sun.

This does not deal with the cause of the problem. It removes what the Chinese call 'excessive chi'. Which just means energy has built up in the wrong place and won't move without a bit of a push!

This tapping pushes the excessive energy away from the place in which it has accumulated. But it does not guarantee where the energy will go to. So people are using this to remove the symptoms their problem creates, but they may be doing so at the expense of some other part of their life.

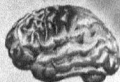

This will show up later if they are lucky. Lucky, because they have a chance to reverse the effect. If it does not show later they could have suppressed the cause of the problem which will mean more serious effects later. It is referred to in different ways but generally accepted as Energy Psychology – or a trick of the trade

This technique is just that – a technique. There is much peripheral information to be obtained from a person about the problem than just to tap some points prescribed because of the type of problem. This is medical thinking, not holistic training. It is far better to use one simple practice that works and let the nervous system learn how to apply that than apply what you know just because it sounds like a good idea.

Everyone is different and these techniques are only at best 'options', not the answers by themselves. Without these practices, though, there is nowhere for other options to 'stick' to the neurology and to be utilised by the subconscious.

FEAR

False Evidence Appearing Real is a great example of an excessive energy reaction. This technique made a name for itself in the early days by eliminating the symptoms of fear, because fear accumulates energy in the kidneys (draining energy from the brain) and using this technique pushes the energy to other places in the body, hence removing the symptoms.

This is one of the greatest techniques for fear but you have to know the right points to tap to bring the whole system back into balance. And because everyone is different, the points needed, will be different from person to person.

I have written a one-day meridian energy workshop teaching the proper way to use this Point Tapping technique, called 'Connecting The Flow',

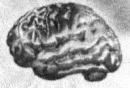

so that you can't do any damage to your energy system or of any other the person's. If you want to know more about that, go to <u>www.TheEfficientCEOBrain.com</u> site and look for 'Connecting The Flow" under the Activation Workshops section.

Exercise Five: Dichotomy Release

This requires tapping two acupuncture areas. The position of these points is really very helpful. They are both located on the hands and very close to each other.

There are a few points on the Small Intestine energy path (Chinese energy meridian) that influence changing the psychological disturbance that stress reactions create. You can tap the whole area along the little finger side of your hand, between the base of the little finger to the beginning of the wrist. (See Illustration below)

There is another point that acts in a similar way to the Small Intestine area called Triple Warmer 3. It's a different pathway of energy that affects the energy going to the head and helps balance the hormonal relationship to stress reactions. (See Illustration below).

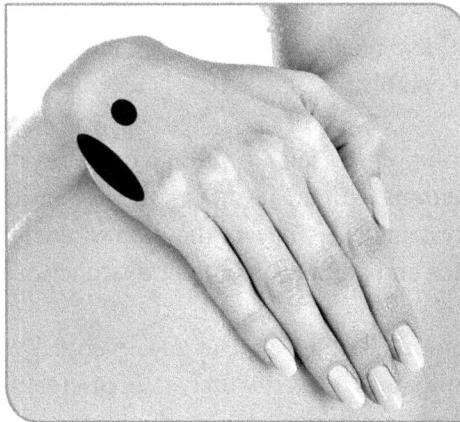

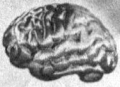

Step by Step

Think of something that stresses you. **Think about what you want to change and tap** first the **TW3** (Small circle on the diagram) Point and then the **Small Intestine Area** (on the side of the hand) while continuing to think of what you want.

Think now of what you do want and tap the two areas.

You can use this technique now with another theme or goal in the same manner as above.

Use the Options Generator and repeat tapping the areas while thinking again of what you want. This can be different than the first time.

Use this technique in conjunction with the other strategies listed in this book.

Emotional reactions can invade every area of your life.

Something goes wrong, to which you have an emotional reaction, and it carries over into other areas of your life that are not relevant to the original challenge at all.

Many of the emotional reactions you feel, are to express emotions which are socially unacceptable.

As a temporary solution so as not to get into deeper waters, you suppress the emotional reactions with the result that they go inside your body, into the organs and systems. This upsets the natural energy balance of the organs and systems and you become more dysfunctional.

Eventually symptoms start to appear and eventually you will try to suppress the symptoms. This is the first stage of creating or activating a more serious disease condition.

Organs and emotions vibrate in concert with each other.

The different organs in your body vibrate in a specific frequency range. The emotions have a frequency range also, and where you suppress an emotion by repressing its expression you push the emotion frequency into the organ/s in your body that have a similar range of frequency.

For example, the vibration of Fear and the vibration of the Kidneys are similar, so Fear sits in the Kidneys when not expressed. Grief has an affinity to the Lungs while Resentment affects the Gall Bladder.

All emotional suppression will lead to the congestion of energy in some gland, organ or system somewhere in your body. One of the first places to get congested is the circulation to the organ, gland or system. Over evolution we have developed a way of 'washing away' the congestion and thereby releasing the stored emotions.

An interesting effect of Neuro-Training is that when blood is stimulated to populate a specific area of the body, any emotions that are caught in that area may come to the surface to be expressed.

Neuro-Vascular Reflexes for deep circulation

Dr Terrence Bennett was a researcher in the USA who discovered a set of reflexes that relate to a special type of circulation (74 beats per minute) that can be stimulated externally to increase blood supply to any specific part of the body.

His research and discoveries led to the use of these points for many types of manual therapies. Its main use has been popularised by Applied Kinesiology and many other types of Kinesiology. We use them here, in Neuro-Training as a way of boosting and clearing any circulation dysfunction.

The result of this work is twofold. Firstly, it increases the flow of blood to various parts of the body, especially the brain. Secondly, it brings nutrition and oxygen to the brain helping it to recuperate and grow more efficiently. The general result is clearer thinking, faster response times, better memory and more efficient thinking under normally 'stressful' situations.

The technique itself is very simple and can be used in most situations and other people don't even know you are balancing your emotional responses to them or the challenges at hand.

This involves 'holding points' on your forehead.

These points are called Neuro-Vascular Points and each one relates to specific organs and muscles in your body. The effect of holding these is to stimulate a deeper circulation to these areas and increase metabolic function, remove congestion and allow nutrients to do their repair work.

This allows your subconscious to rearrange and clean up the mess you make by dumping emotions and other 'unwanteds' in your body.

Yes, that's right. We all do this.

You use our body as a dumping ground for the things you don't want to know about or think you can't fix anyway. You hold these 'events' in your body with congestion. You congest an area to hold an unwanted emotion in that area. If you reverse the congestion, the things trapped in there are released to be processed in a more appropriate way, hopefully.

These points show conclusively that there are physiological actions you can take to induce neurological changes. These in turn, change function of specific or general areas of your body and how they function.

This means if you know where to stimulate and in what best way to stimulate, you can train your nervous system to do what you want it to do.

Firstly, there is an education process you must go through to be able to accept the emotions these techniques will bring to the surface. This happens a lot faster if you can identify what the emotions are.

You will probably be aware of your Emotional Reaction areas because these are the emotions you feel at any stress time and are usually more defence-related. Any emotional reaction conducted over extended periods of time will become habitual. At the earliest stage of experiencing any of these emotions, you would have been conscious of their existence, even if by now you have desensitised yourself to them.

Exercise Six: Emotion Exchange

The Emotional Exchange process is to find the existing emotional states and associate in a new, stronger and more supportive emotional state. This is done by holding the points illustrated on the diagram below and following the instructions.

1. Decide the theme, topic or stress reaction you wish to change your response to.

2. Hold the points indicated in the diagram and continue to hold these through the whole exercise.

3. Hold the thoughts until you can't hold them any longer before going to the next step.

4. Think intensely about the stress reaction until it seems to change or disappear.

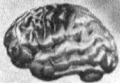

5. Think of how you would like the situation to be and identify some marker that tells you the situation has changed. For example, you may imagine your boss/husband/wife/friend/enemy/ or doctor giving you a big smile.

6. Add something fantastic and new to your vision of the situation, imagining that it is even better than before. Ask yourself, "What could I do to make it better?" Do that now! Remember you can add any new emotional state you want here as well.

7. Imagine this new vision in your life. How is affecting all those near to you? Does it in anyway limit you or anyone else? If so, change it to something even better that helps you and the others. When satisfied that you can't make it any better, imagine it in every part of who you are, inside and out.

8. Imagine what you are like in ten years from now having made these changes. Look back towards now and see how you did all those new things. How does that make you feel?

    If you feel not so good, go back to point 4 and find the other people you forgot to include before. Continue through the process until you are doing this point (8) again. Keep going through this cycle until you feel GOOD at this stage.

9. Take this good feeling and give it a colour, shape, sound and position inside you. Make the good feeling even stronger by giving it the ability to go through every part of 'who you are', increasing the intensity of colour and sound. Breathe the way you would breathe if that good feeling was 100 times stronger and continue to breathe that way until you feel the emotion and its colour, in every part of you.

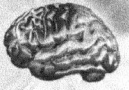

Enjoy the process and notice what things change in your life. It is automatic and will often surprise you that your response will have changed so radically.

Repeat this process with the next stress reaction. Enjoy!

Below is the illustration of the positions of the Neuro-Vascular Points you hold while doing this process. You will get a little more benefit if you use two or more fingers on the positions illustrated.

Hold these points for sixty seconds while going through the whole of the process above.

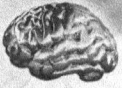

SECTION 4: FIXATION RELEASE

This technique is specifically directed towards the physical effect of continued stress reactions.

When you have had a long duration of stress reactions, you tend to stiffen and tighten all the ligaments and tendons, which is a consequence of the change of adrenal hormones and especially reduction of the mineral-corticoids produced by the adrenal glands.

As compensation to this physical state, you 'hold on' to all the structural parts too strongly. This creates what is called 'fixations' between the bones in your body. The area affected most by this phenomena are the cranial bones and spinal vertebrae. There is still some contention in some areas as to whether the cranial bones move or not. Yet there is plenty of observable evidence to prove that they do move naturally and cause problems if they can't move.

Whether this technique changes the motion of the cranial bones or any other bones does not really matter. So long as the movement of the bones that are not operating properly because of the long-term effect of stress reactions is changed, you will get more freedom of movement and sense of easiness inside you.

Neurologically this allows better and more efficient nerve activity to control the various physical functions that are changed when you are in the middle of a stress reaction.

The mechanism that maintains these 'fixations' of the bones is controlled by the Pineal Gland. Commonly known for its regulation of hormonal rhythms within your body, it is also dependant on certain minerals for its function.

The Pineal Gland lives on natural light

When this gland cannot get the normal, necessary amount of light, it eats its second preference food, which is magnesium. It gets the magnesium by tensing the muscles that would normally hold the bones together (usually in the spine) and therefore reduces the amount of magnesium available for normal nervous function related to that bone junction.

The free magnesium is then used by the Pineal Gland while it has insufficient light to feed on. This is effectively how a fixation is created and may even become a habitual response. This should only be a limited and temporary response but can become habituated into being a normal response to stress reactions. It is here that your physical body becomes susceptible to physical damage.

To reverse this state, you need to feed the Pineal Gland the foods it prefers, light.

To do that is very easy. Simply shine a pen torch, (battery operated hand held torch (flashlight)) so it shines on the pineal area of the front of the skull. This is just above and between the eyebrows.

This effectively makes the Pineal Gland release the hold on the muscles and the magnesium can be used again in the nervous system. The fixation is released and the muscles and bone joints can move as they want.

An enormous amount of recuperation can take place once the joints are operating more efficiently. This is a very easy and quick influence on the nervous system and hormones and allows a lot of physical problems to be avoided. It is better to do this before and after any physical exercise to protect against any damage from straining or excessive training.

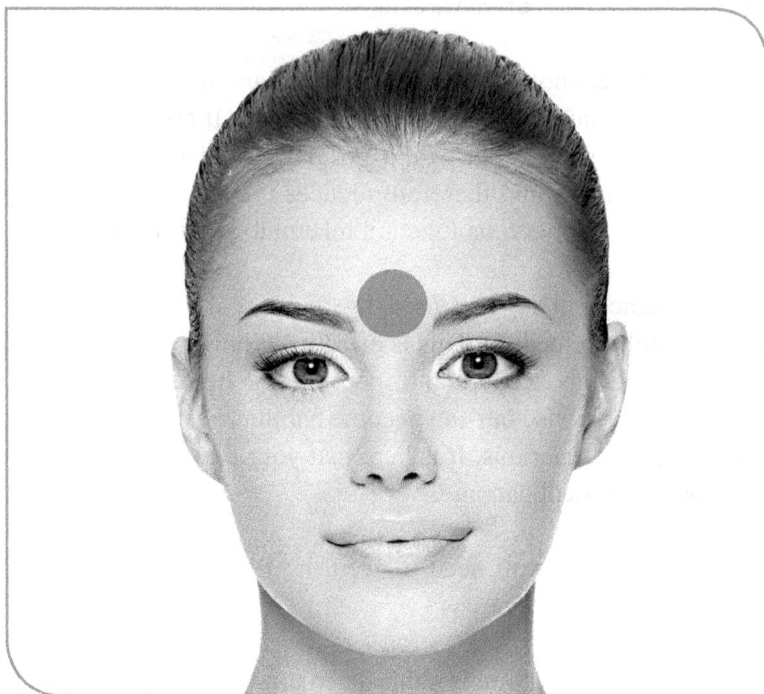

Exercise Seven: The Fixation Technique

1. Decide on the stress reaction you wish to change.

2. Shine the flashlight on your forehead for about 60 seconds between the eyebrows, as illustrated.

3. Continue to think of the stress reaction until you can't think of it any more.

4. Move your body around while still shining the flashlight and thinking of your stress reaction.

5. Imagine the first time you felt this reaction and move your body while shining the light.

6. Anchor yourself back in present time awareness with a big in breath.

7. Repeat the process for the next stress reaction. Note: If you have difficulty moving for some reason, just make small movements until you can increase them at a later stage.

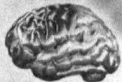

SECTION 5 – YOUR FUTURE

Some nice philosophies

Physiological and psychological effects of stress are common. It is a generally accepted idea that stress causes physiological changes that are detrimental to your health. Well, it must follow that anything that reverses that stress must at least stop the detrimental effects of stress and may even help to overcome the damage it has done.

I would suggest that the techniques I have given you in this book will do both those things and more. The right type of stress strategy will not only 'stop the rot' from the stress reactions but will also help you to recuperate in ways which are specific for your nervous and something that your subconscious cannot refuse.

The question still remains, "What do you do about your future?"

I have a few nice concepts that may help you with your future and your relationship to it.

The empty cup

This is a simple story of the apprentice who comes to the master asking for the master to teach him everything he knows. The master tells the apprentice to pour tea into a tea cup. The apprentice is annoyed by this as he wants to know the secrets to the master's wisdom.

The master said calmly, "Keep pouring." The apprentice proclaimed that the cup was filing up. The master said "Keep pouring." The apprentice kept pouring the tea until it spilled over the edge of the cup and burnt his hand. He was very angry with the master and asked why he had told

him to do something that would harm him. The master answered calmly, "When you come to me for knowledge, make sure you empty your cup first so that you can take away as much knowledge as you can bear."

The lesson in this for us is, when you think you know everything, you stop yourself from seeing the things you don't know and the possibility of learning more. Come to any interaction with the concept of listening to fill your empty cup with the knowledge you get from others.

Apply the knowledge in your own time respecting that knowledge may come at times least expected and your stress reactions to not knowing fast enough will simply disappear.

Learn to fish

A principle that has helped me to define my place in life has been the story of learning how to fish.

If I were to give a man a fish to satisfy his hunger, he would be satisfied for only a short time and he would be hungry again very soon. If I was to give the man the knowledge of how to fish and spent time with him to confirm his ability to fish, he will never be hungry again. Giving a person the ability to be self-reliant, gives you freedom to go and teach others how to fish. The man can feed himself and those he is responsible for and you can be responsible for the value of your knowledge.

Personal discipline

One of the real advantages of being who you are is that you are not a static fixed entity that cannot change.

In fact, you cannot not change. So why don't you change in the way that would produce the best results in your life?

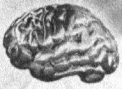

There are some simple concepts you can train yourself into the type of person you want to be. All of them depend on your ability to turn them into rituals or habits that support positive productive behaviours.

Practice concentration

There are a number of activities you can exercise your concentration with. Anything you do will be an opportunity to practice your concentration ability.

Read well, focus with clarity and attention on what you are doing all the time and be aware of yourself in the process.

Do not let your ego take control of what you are doing. Know you are in full control of your actions and if you want to stop doing something, then stop.

Time yourself

Make a time for everything and stick to those times with no excuses for changing them.

Wake at the same time every morning and go to bed at the same time every night.

Discipline yourself to work on a project for a definite period of time that you decide on, then stop when that time has come. This will give you a measure of your day and a better way to organise your talents.

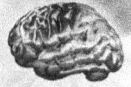

Reimagine yourself

Never believe that you are not able to achieve what you want.

Always practice thinking of how you would (not could) do something better. Ask yourself, "How would I do this better?" Create a picture of yourself inside your mind that you can access any time. Go into the picture and start changing things around till you are happy with them. How they function, what they do for you and others.

Ask again, "How would I make this better?"

Now to make the image a part of who you are there are a couple of steps you need to follow.

Affirm your desired state

Think about the image of yourself you just created and make a statement affirming that from now on this is the pattern or model you follow. e.g., "I am this new image from this time on".

Visualise the successful achievement of your goal

Your new image needs to be able to DO something for you. It needs to be achieving something you want in your life. Make it something like a quality or talent rather than a material item. Imagine the new image creating the goals you want to achieve with even greater results. Visualise yourself achieving the goals. Feel the feelings or emotions associated with achieving your goal.

Pay attention to the emotions you feel while achieving your goals. If they don't feel too good, go back to the visualisation and look for the element that needs to change. Make the changes and resample the emotional response.

When the emotions are good, amplify them to their extremes by breathing the way you would if the emotion was ten times stronger. Feel the colour of the emotion moving through every part of 'who you are' till all of you is bathed in the emotion.

Look for more positive emotions to go through this process and continue until you cannot find anymore emotions to amplify.

Exercise Eight: Fear Destruction. This Is Important- Pay Attention

Fear is based on misperception

If you have the wrong perception or perceive that something is trying to threaten our existence, you go into an automatic response to survive. If this becomes habituated, you become driven by fear rather than by common sense.

One of the unfortunate things about living our lives based on fear is it suppresses the emotional states you want to have. While you exercise fear you will never feel the way you want to. This is why fear and depression are always linked. The fear makes us unable to feel the way you want which adds more evidence that you can never have what you want.

My experience of working with depressive and stressed individuals has been that there is only one reality filter that is stronger than fear.

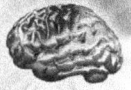

If you destroy the fear, you can redirect the energy it consumes and use it to create what you want.

I am going to show you now the way to overcome fear so it cannot influence you again and how you can convert its energy into a resource.

Destroy the FEAR.

Below is a simple formula for identifying and destroying any fear.

All fears are based on or create 'needs'.

The first thing to do is make a list of all the 'needs' around what is stressing or depressing you.

1. **Identify The Need.**

   Ask yourself "What do I need to not have ****?"

   Make a list of these needs and work with each one in the same way.

2. **Determine the Fear behind not having that 'Need'.**

   Ask yourself this question, "What am I afraid of if I can't have this 'state the need'?"

3. **Picture That Fear.**

   Give the fear a colour and a shape and feel where it is inside you.

   Decide to be free from the fear and imagine it outside your body, in front of you.

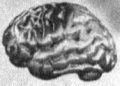

4. **Destroy The Fear.**

Destroy the fear so it can never come back. You can imagine burning, exploding, vaporising or doing anything else to destroy the fear.

Ask yourself, "Can it come back?" If not, you have destroyed it. If it can, think again of how to destroy it.

5. **Exaggerate The Resulting Positive Emotion.**

Once the fear is destroyed, feel what it's like to not have the fear. If it is a positive emotion, amplify it by imagining it's 100 times stronger. Breathe the way you would breathe if it was the strongest emotion in the world.

For example: Person 'X' has a pain in the left side of the chest.

Q. "What do you NEED to not have the pain?"

A. "To feel more relaxed". (Being relaxed is the need)

Q. "What are you AFRAID OF if you cannot be relaxed?"

A. "That I'll have a heart attack."! (The FEAR is that of having a heart attack.)

Sensory Input

Qs. "What colour would that fear be?"

"What shape would that fear be?"

"What Weight would that fear be?"

"Does it have an odour?"

"Does it have a temperature?"

"Does it have three dimensions?" "

"Where does that fear live inside you?"

Continue until a clear picture is obtained.

Now, **destroy the fear**. Shoot it. Dissolve it. Cast a spell on it. Explode it.

Do whatever it takes to destroy that fear, so it can't come back.

Note: The fear MUST be destroyed. Only complete elimination of the fear will allow the emotion it was suppressing to become accessible again.

Q. "What do you feel, not having that fear?"

A. "Relaxed"

"Multiply that feeling by 10 or 100 times" "How would you be breathing?" "Breathe that way now."

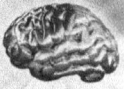

Anchor the positive state

Now give that feeling a symbol and imagine using it in the situations where you had encountered the fear in the past. Notice the difference of the feeling and focus on it in present time with that symbol. This process necessarily infers that you have the ability to be free from the limitations and restrictions that come from the fears that plague your subconscious.

The goals you previously aspired to can now be changed into something relating to your wants rather than your needs.

Put these two procedures into practice and experience for yourself what these can do to revalue your life experiences and therefore change depression into personal freedom.

www.TheEfficientCEOBrain.com

Author Profile

ANDREW VERITY

Author, Master Neuro-Trainer, Entrepreneur, Kinesiology researcher and Practitioner

Andrew is an author, Master Neuro-Trainer, entrepreneur, highly trained Kinesiology researcher and practitioner.

Energised by his lifelong passion for understanding neurological health, Andrew is the founder and director of Neuro-Training Pty Ltd which serves as the foundation for a growing international network of schools offering diplomas in Neuro-Training and Kinesiology throughout Australia, Norway, Germany, Italy, South Africa, and Switzerland.

In Australia, Andrew is the director of Neuro-Training and the College of Neuro-Training where he focuses on research and development of Neuro-Training techniques which become course content. The college has three campuses in Victoria, three in New South Wales, two in Western Australia, and one in South Australia. Additionally, Andrew conducts training in the corporate arena, high net worth individual and royal family consulting, where he focuses on the practical applications of Neuroscience for business and life improvement combined with the natural and alternative human sciences with Kinesiology as its base.

During his six-year term as the President of the International Association of Specialised Kinesiologists, Andrew aided in laying the groundwork for professional structures of qualifications that are now the accepted norm, both in Australia and internationally.

In his youth, Andrew was an active athlete with interests in Judo, squash, running, weight training, basketball, and Australian Rules football. Having earned his black belt in Judo, he competed for many years and won the Australian Judo Championship.

Andrew credits his athletic success to the 'weird techniques' he learned from a publication his father gave him from the International College of Applied Kinesiology. After using those techniques to strengthen his muscles far beyond what he was able to accomplish with weight training, Andrew made it his mission to continue to advance the science of Neuro-Training. He enrolled in a Naturopathic college and earned simultaneous diplomas in Homeopathy, Naturopathy, and Iridology.

After founding his one-man Kinesiology and Naturopathic practice, Andrew continued to learn everything he could, and he began training others in the United States, Europe, and Australia. All of his efforts have helped Kinesiology and Neuro-Training rise in popularity around the world.

Andrew has written more than 36 public education manuals and more than 30 Neuro-Training manuals for the delivery of a diploma in Neuro-Training as well as advanced training. When he isn't integrating new developments into Neuro-Training, Andrew enjoys graphic design, 'weird science stuff', Judo, Aikido, and life.

Andrew Verity ND, DH, DI, MNT, AP is the author of *The Efficient CEO Brain* and lives in Victoria, Australia.

Recommended
Resources

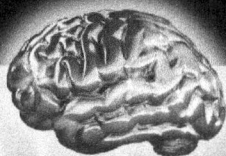

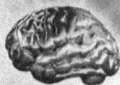

Recommended Resources

Activation Workshops to fine tune
your Nervous System and Brain.

TRAIN YOUR BRAIN
BY TRAINING YOUR NERVOUS SYSTEM

**A series of Workshops and DVD Training to
reorganise fundamental processing in your nervous
system and brain**

Gives Your Mind the Foundation – To Do Miracles

Hands-on techniques you can follow by the number and train
yourself to become subtly powerful.

Developed over decades of research, these workshops are the
basis of a healthy wealthy and wise nervous system that is
implemented consciously for your subconscious to use when
it needs to.

If you want the ability to manage better your physical, emotional
and even mental responses to life experiences, we have a way
out of the stress and into the freedom to design your life by
choice. We are proud to present this new approach so you can
experience 'first hand' its power to help you be the best person
you can be.

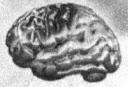

Learn how your body is organised from the molecular level to a systems level is what we do best. We understand just what you need to know and do, to overcome those seemingly impossible challenges.

If you could expand your awareness wouldn't that increase the quality of your life as well? We will show you the answers you already have inside you. We help you to find the right connection to the resources you already have.

We invite you to participate in one or all of our Activation Programs, taught at the Neuro-Training Centre for you to experience and bring more value into your life.

If you are a Parent or planning to become one, Student, Professional in the health care or personal development industry, you should come to a presentation, class or workshop and get the right solutions for your life and your business. See you at a free presentation.

Contact us now for details at:
andrew@theefficientceobrain.com

Adaptive Neurology Workshops

HEALTH AND WEALTH CREATION FROM THE INSIDE-OUT WITH HANDS ON TRAINING

A new approach to health and wealth creation through the specific use of human neurological phenomena that will revolutionise the personal development industry

Your body has a wonderful operating system we call nerves. With this training you can learn how to use an amazing phenomenon to reorganise specific conditioning that limits your nervous system's ability.

We have three basic Workshops and other advancing training is offered regularly for to enjoy adding new knowledge to your neurology.

This is all totally natural and doesn't require any external interventions to make it happen. This is a way of reforming the internal function to gain advantage with your innate abilities and innate systems.

For anyone who has any type of challenge to overcome, or who just wants to be better. You don't have to be sick to become better.

If you want to become a major force in the health care industry, a thought leader in your consulting or just a person with an amazing ability to help others really reach their potential, this is for you!

Contact us at andrew@theefficientceobrain.com

For the dates of the basic workshops.

Book in for a free presentation, come and ask as many questions as you like and find out for yourself what potential this has for you.

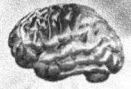

Professional Qualification Training

EVEN IF YOU HAVE HEARD OF KINESIOLOGY, NATUROPATHY, HOMEOPATHY OR OTHER NATURAL THERAPIES, YOU NEED NOT LOOK ANY FURTHER!

A full government recognised Diploma in Kinesiology as well as a Diploma of Neuro-Training is offered by Neuro-Training P/L,

a Registered Training Organization (RTO).

This is a unique qualification that trains you how to become a practitioner in Neuro-Training and Kinesiology and is recognised in institutions internationally as well as in four states of Australia.

The Diploma of Kinesiology and Neuro-Training integrates the Principles of other proven health Modalities within a working session format that has been developed over decades of experimentation and research.

Hundreds of practitioners and thousands of clients have experienced the amazing benefits of this unique modality.

If you are looking for a legitimate and powerful way of making a difference in the world, if you want to become a professionally recognised influence for change in people's life experience, you must consider this as a career of choice.

I have seen many lives changed in the most profound way using this modality that it's difficult to explain what it's like. My first secretary used to say, "Well what does a strawberry taste like?" the answer was always, "You have to taste it yourself."

Go to College of Neuro-Training.
www.collegeofneuro-training.edu.au